UP YOUR
S.A.T. SCORE

UP YOUR S.A.T. SCORE

THE UNDERGROUND GUIDE TO PSYCHING OUT THE SCHOLASTIC APTITUDE TEST

BY LARRY BERGER, MANEK MISTRY, AND PAUL ROSSI

NEW CHAPTER PRESS INC., NEW YORK

Library of Congress Catalog Card Number: 87-61127

ISBN 0-942257-00-6

SAT questions selected from *5 SATs,* 1984, *6 SATs,* 1982, *10 SATs,* 1983, *10 SATs,* 1986 College Entrance Examination Board. Reprinted by permission of Educational Testing Service, the copyright owner of the test questions.

Permission to reprint the SAT material does not constitute review or endorsement by Educational Testing Service or the College Board of this publication as a whole or of any other testing information it may contain.

SAT and Scholastic Aptitude Test are registered trademarks of the College Entrance Examination Board.

Grateful acknowledgment is made for permission to reprint the following:
"DE DO DO DO, DE DA DA DA" (Sting). © 1980 Virgin Music (Publishers) Ltd. Published in the USA/Canada by Virgin Music Inc. All Rights Reserved. Used by permission.
"Kiss" by Prince. © 1986 Controversy Music.
"You Can Call Me Al" by Paul Simon. ©1986 Paul Simon Music.

Designed by Barbara Marks
Cover photograph by Arthur Klonsky/Janeart
Evil Testing Serpent drawn by Paul Selwyn

TO OUR PARENTS
FLORENCE AND TOBY BERGER
CHARLINE AND FAUST ROSSI
VIRGINIA AND NARIMAN MISTRY

ACKNOWLEDGMENTS

There are many people who have helped us with *Up Your Score.* Listed in alphabetical order, the following people deserve our deep gratitude.

Elizabeth Berger, for her medical consultation for the "Little Circles" chapter;

Florence Berger, professor of management at the Cornell University School of Hotel Administration, for helping with the memory and concentration chapters, and for revealing her secret recipe for Sweet and Tasty 800 Bars;

Toby Berger, electrical engineering professor at Cornell University, for calculating the statistics that prove our methods work, advising us on the math section, and correcting our mistayckes;

Ken Blanchard, for suggesting that we send our manuscript to New Chapter Press;

David Bock, Ithaca High School, for being a terrific math teacher, for the valuable ideas he gave us for the guessing section, and for his editing assistance;

Belle Cohen, for her good counsel, and the use of her home and telephone;

Randy A. Faigin, for her suggestions and her terrific supportiveness;

Dennis Ferguson, for his excellent proofreading of our initial manuscript;

The Ferndale, California Focus Group: Michael Laris, Ryan Dixon, Dawn Eastin, Casey Laris, and Jenny Russell, for their early enthusiasm for the book;

Nous remercions bien cordialement les Fougerays d'avoir si aimablement hebergé Paul tout au long de l'année dernière;

Florence Harris, for her generous editing assistance and advice;

Lynn C. Harris, freshperson at Yale, for her extraordinary support, outstanding advice, and hilarious contributions;

All of our friends in the Ithaca High School Class of '86 for their encouragement and suggestions;

Milton Kagan, one of the few SAT coaches who really knows his stuff, for sharing some of his excellent ideas with us;

Andrea Kochie, Ithaca High School, for being an amazing college admissions advisor, and for helping us acquire so much of the information that we needed;

Tamara Lange, for her support and encouragement;

Kevin McMahon, Ithaca High School math teacher, for his suggestions about the math section;

The people at New Chapter Press—Wendy Crisp, Kathryn Arnold, Mary Tooley and Kate Walker—for deciding to publish our book, for putting up with three neophyte co-authors, and for being a joy to work with;

James Pullman, amazing English teacher at IHS, for helping us plan the TSWE section;

Faust and Charline Rossi, for the many kind efforts they have made on our behalf;

Steve Wendelboe, director of athletics, New Palestine High School, New Palestine, Indiana for his support; and

The Yale Class of '90: Deborah Bloom, Amelia Eisch, David Franklin, James Hanaham, Chris Kincade, Julian Kleindorfer, Andrew Michaelson, Jim Rosenfeld, Zachary Silverstein, and SM 1845J for their contributions, humor, and support.

CONTENTS

A Brief History of How This Book Came to Be

This book really bites the monstrous one," Paul yawned as he pulled the crust off his sandwich, scattering Miracle Whip all over page 12 of the Barron's SAT guide.

"Yeah, what's the point of the SAT anyway?"

"To cause us pain and suffering," Manek mumbled.

"You know what's wrong with all these SAT review books?"

"No, what?" asked Larry.

"They're all written by embalmed educators who were born before the invention of the number 2 pencil, before the SAT itself, and before they took Tang to the moon."

"If I could write an SAT review book, it wouldn't be so boring."

"I know what you mean. If I wrote an SAT review book it would be one that was erudite, and yet not bombastic, one that would comprehensively elucidate the turbid depths of this baneful examination, one that would carry students to new heights of academic self-actualization, one that would. . ."

"Yeah, and one with lots of skin."

"No, Larry's right. If we could write a kick-ass manual telling confused, bored, and sexually frustrated students like us across this great land how to rock on the SAT we would—"

"Yes indeed, we would be providing a contribution to society that. . ."

". . .that could bring us enough funds to pay for college."

". . .and a chance to get on Letterman."

"Letterman? Do you really think so?"

"Sure, why not?"

And so, a few months later, after Larry, Manek, and Paul had each earned SAT scores over 1500, they began work on an SAT review book that would share the secrets of their SAT success with their fellow students. A book that will help you, too, get into one of those colleges that costs more than you can afford.

ABOUT THE SAT

Good question. Let's face it—life is rough and sludge colored. Why bother with all this studying when you can always get a job doing some kind of unskilled labor? There are many exciting job opportunities for people who don't do well on the SAT. For example, the phone company is always looking for people to work as dial tones. The only prerequisite for employment is that you can hold the same pitch 24 hours a day without inhaling.

If, however, you do not have perfect pitch, and you still want to apply to college, your last hope is to read this book.

Why do I have to read this book if I want to go to college?

If you don't already know, then we *strongly* suggest that you consider the unskilled labor alternative mentioned above.

What is the SAT?

The SAT, Scholastic Aptitude Test, was developed in 1927 because colleges wanted an objective way of comparing students. It used to be that they had no way of knowing that Eggbert's D average at Impossible High School was actually much more impressive than Buffy's B average at Easy Academy. Supposedly, the SAT will give an accurate measure of a student's ability to do college work. Certain teenage review book authors think that it fails miserably in its attempt to do this, but the fact remains that it is a very important part of your college application. Your SAT score can make the difference between acceptance to and rejection from a college.

No, really, what is the SAT?

A good combined score (math plus verbal) is 1600; a bad combined score is 400. Again, if you have problems with this see the section about unskilled labor.

What is a "good score" on the SAT?

Well, that depends. First, you have to consider what you plan to use your score for. Some of you are reading this book because the new NCAA rules require that you get a composite score of 700 in order to be eligible to play

No, seriously, what score should I shoot for?

on an intercollegiate team as a freshman. Some of you want to score in the 1500s to ensure your place at Harvard. The table below gives the average 1986 SAT scores at a wide variety of schools.

School	Verbal SAT	Math SAT	Combined Scores
Amherst	640	670	1310
UCLA	490	560	1050
University of Connecticut	500	550	1050
Georgetown	630	650	1280
Harvard	680	700	1380
Indiana University	460	510	970
Idaho State	430	473	903
Kent State	430	470	900
MIT	650	740	1390
Stanford	620	670	1290
Tufts	580	640	1220
Yale	660	680	1340
University of Utah	500	500	1000

These scores are the average scores. They are typical of the scores of the students entering these schools. They are not minimum requirements, nor do they guarantee your admission.

*Legacy is having relatives who went to the school you are applying to. We asked Jim Wroth, a sophomore at Yale, what he got on the SAT, and he said 1760. When we responded that it's impossible to score above 1600, he explained that he has Yale relatives who date back to the year 1760, so it didn't really matter what his scores were.

There are many other considerations in gaining admission to college. High school grades, work experience, application essays, leadership qualities, the admissions interview, ethnic background, legacy,* and many other things all have an impact on whether or not you get in. If you are president of every club in your school, the admissions officers may be so impressed with your extracurricular activities that they'll accept you even if you scored noticeably below the school's average SAT score. But if you don't have legacy and you have a boring list of extracurriculars, then you will need SAT scores well above the average scores.

Although these other factors all are important, none of them is as crucial as a student's SAT score. Many admissions officers would try to deny that claim, but the admissions records show that if you have an SAT score above the average for the school to which you are applying, and there's nothing flagrantly wrong with the rest of your application, then you will almost certainly get in. While the other factors on your applications are subjective, your SAT score is a big, fat, hairy, objective *number*. Even an admissions officer who claims that the SAT score is not particularly important is going to be subconsciously influenced by this number. It categorizes your application in the admissions officer's mind as "smart kid" or "dumb kid." It has an impact on the way an admissions officer interprets virtually everything else on your application.

If you've already taken the PSAT and you didn't study for it, don't read this. It will only depress you.

What about the PSAT?

A PSAT is the same as an SAT except that (1) there is no Test of Standard Written English on it, and (2) there is just one 50 minute math section and one 50 minute verbal section instead of the two 30 minute math and two 30 minute verbal sections that are on the SAT. Another difference is that, while SAT does not have a *P* as its first letter, PSAT does. Here's why. . .

The *P* in PSAT stands for three things. The first is easy—*P*reliminary. The PSAT is a preliminary look at the real SAT. It's a sneak preview of what the real thing is going to be like and a good chance to practice.

But the PSAT is more than just a chance to practice. The second thing the *P* stands for is Scholarshi*p*s and S*p*ecial *P*rograms. A good score on the PSAT makes you eligible for all sorts of swell scholarship programs, the most famous of which is the National Merit Scholarship Program. The National Merit Scholarship is based on your *selection index*, which is your math score plus twice your verbal score. Recognition by the National Merit Program is a big plus on your college applications and it can even win you some money. The top 50,000 scorers are recognized by the Merit Program. The top 15,000 scorers become semifinalists. Out of the top 15,000 they pick 13,500 to become finalists. About 6,000 of the finalists get big bucks towards college. This program is described in-depth in the "PSAT/NMSQT Student Bulletin" which you can pick up in any guidance counselor's office.

PSAT scores are also a factor in determining many other scholarships as well, including Negro Students Fund, Telluride, and Hispanic Scholar awards. The list of scholarships using the PSAT score is published in *Winning Money for College: The High School Student's Guide to Scholarship Contests* by Alan Deutschman.

The third thing the *P* stands for ·is A*pp*lications. The Educational Testing Service (ETS), the company that writes the tests, publishes a pamphlet on taking the PSAT that says the PSAT is not used as a college admission test. But, some schools have a space for PSAT scores on their applications. Other times there will just be a space where you can put "other test scores." Of course, it's optional whether or not you tell them your PSAT scores, but it's impressive if you have good ones. Also, they *know* that you took the PSAT. So, if you don't want to put your PSAT scores on the application, they will suspect that your scores were poor.

What special skills will I need to take the SAT?

A variety of abilities are necessary. First, you must be able to stay awake, which can be difficult even though you will be sitting for three hours in the most uncomfortable chair imaginable. (This is why we have included sections on yoga and concentration.) Second, you must be able to read. (And if you're reading this, you've probably already cleared that hurdle.) Third, you must know a lot of math and verbal stuff so that you can answer the questions correctly. (That's what most of this book is about.) Fourth, you need to understand the proper strategies for taking the SAT and the many ways that you can outsmart the test. (We explain all of the tricks.) Fifth, after you find the right answer, you need to be able to fill in all the little circles on the computerized answer sheet, without going out of the lines. (We've provided several pages of little circles for practice and have done extensive experimentation on what is the most efficient way to fill them in.)

Other useful skills are food smuggling and secretive eating. These skills are covered in this book's final section.

You cannot study for the SAT unless you are mentally and physically prepared. Listed below are several ways of psyching yourself up for the SAT.

How do I get psyched to study for the SAT?

1. Try to convince yourself that it is fun and challenging to learn new words and mathematical facts. Oh well, nice try.
2. Next, try to convince yourself that the things you learn in today's study session will enable you to think critically and to appear intelligent and to sound articulate for the rest of your life. This technique does not work either.
3. Realize that the opposite sex is often attracted to equations and big words. Nope.
4. Note that the average teenager will burn approximately 115 calories during an hour of intense studying. Maybe so, but walking up and down stairs for an hour is much more interesting and burns 350 calories.

The above techniques do not work because they use positive thinking. The SAT does not inspire positive thinking. You must learn to think negatively. For example:

1. Recognize that if you do not do well on the SAT you will not get into a good college. You will have to go to college in the Yukon Territory and your college years will be disrupted by glacial migrations.
2. Go to the kitchen. Turn on the blender to high speed. Then, insert your hand and try to stop the blade. By comparison, studying for the SAT may actually be pleasurable.
3. Realize that the ETS is a wicked organization. By reading our book you are beating its system and you will score higher than you would otherwise.

4. Most of the dweebs who deserve to get into the college of their choice are probably too busy programming their computers to have time to read this book. It's fun to watch dweebs get mad when they don't get into a college that you get into.
5. The SAT is expensive:

$11.50	test fee
$ 9.95	this book
$ 8.95	*10 SATs*
$ 1.00	gas to and from test
$ 0.40	four #2 pencils
$ 4.00	food smuggled into test
$35.80	Total

You don't want to waste that kind of money.

You must learn to dwell on these negative thoughts. Let them gnaw at your insides. Begin to feel a hatred of this test and all that it stands for. Hate is a powerful emotion: It will give you the necessary drive and determination needed for intense study.

An Authors' Note intended to build your confidence

Before we begin we must make one important point. In the extremely unlikely event that you read this book and still do miserably on the SAT, do not whine. Just make the best of going to college in the Yukon Territory. There are a number of small details that could go wrong during the test regardless of what you learn (or do not learn) from this book. A few examples:

1. You lose your admission ticket so they never even let you into the testing center.
2. You fall asleep during the reading comprehension passage about the history of celery.
3. You fall asleep while the proctor is reading the directions.
4. You fall asleep the night before the test and do not wake up until the test is over.
5. You don't know the answer to question number 6 on the test, so you skip it. However, you forget to leave

number 6 blank on your answer sheet. Then, you put the answer to number 7 in the space for number 6, the answer to number 8 in the space for number 7, etc. You don't realize that you have done this until you wake up from the passage about the history of celery and try to find your place. Actually, if you mess up your answer sheet like that, the proctor will probably give you some time to rearrange your answers after the test is over. Raise your hand and ask.

6. Your skateboard breaks.

Sometimes, however, distractions during the test can be remedied. For example, if your desk squeaks, or if it's too hot, or if there's a fan that's blowing your papers away, or if you're left-handed and the desks are made for right-handed people—tell the proctor! Although some proctors bite, most don't carry any dangerous diseases, and an occasional proctor will even try to help you. (See "Proctors: Mindless Slaves of the ETS" in Section 6.)

There is much disagreement about the ideal way to prepare for the SAT. Each of the authors of this book has his own favorite method. Choose the one that is best suited to your lifestyle.

How should I prepare the day before the SAT?

Preparedness is the key. Have a healthy breakfast of juice, toast, milk, and organic cereal. Walk briskly to school so that you have time to giggle with your friends and clean your teacher's blackboard. Pay attention in all your classes. Go to the Honor Society meeting. While you are at varsity track practice, try your hardest to demonstrate your dedication to the coach and your pride in the school. Go home. Do your homework. Spend the night before the test relaxing—see a movie, listen to a comedy record, practice your clarinet, play Truth or Dare. Don't bother with last minute studying except to look at your list of the 10 words that have given you the most trouble. Collect four number 2 pencils with unblemished erasers,

1. LARRY'S METHOD: PREPAREDNESS

your ID, and your admission ticket and put them by the door. Say your prayers, and go to bed early.

2. MANEK'S METHOD: TRANQUILITY

Tranquility is the key. That's what they said to Michael Jackson when his hair caught on fire. And it's true—be tranquil. Skip school the day before and relax—take the phone off the hook, lock the door, and put a cloth over your goldfish bowl so that you won't be distracted. Lie down on the floor with your favorite potato and breathe deeply. Starting with your toes and progressing to your earlobes, calm your entire body; feel yourself losing control of your muscles. When you're marvelously mellow, put your most prized possessions in the microwave and melt them. If you feel alarmed at this stage, then you're not totally tranquil—go back to the beginning and start over again.

When you are entirely free of tension, center your thoughts on how wonderful it will feel to be done with the test, while pronouncing solemn and meditative syllables of wisdom. Close your eyes. Sleep.

3. PAUL'S METHOD: ADRENALINE

Adrenaline is the key. Do not prepare for the SAT the day before. Instead, try to build up as much anxiety and fury as possible in your tortured, nerve-racked body. Do calisthenics. Thrash to loud music. Invite a few friends over and engage in a primal screaming session. Then, beat your body repeatedly with knotted cords and whips. Break lots of glass. When morning comes, make sure that your pulse is above 250 beats per minute, then break open the testing center doors and destroy the test with your awesome animal energy.

It is a myth that organizing materials such as your pencils, ID, admission ticket, and prayer manual the night before improves your score or general well-being. Disorganization forces you to think fast and deal rationally with unusual situations and problems. It is good final preparation for those tricky questions that will undoubtedly appear on the SAT. Finally, don't go to sleep the night before the test. Spend the wee hours of the morning furiously cramming for the next day. You can catch up on your sleep the first year you're dead.

Each method has its merits. People using the first method tend to get higher scores, people using the second method get the most spiritual enrichment from the test, and people using the third method tend to die young. No matter which method you use, be sure to read the wisdom on the last page of this book on the night before the test. Don't peek at it before then.

Who makes up the SAT?

The accepted answer to this question is that it is made up by the Educational Testing Service, a company based in New Jersey. However, we have discovered that this answer is a cover-up. The real truth about who makes up the SAT is revealed here for the first time in history.

THE STORY OF THE EVIL TESTING SERPENT

In the beginning, there was no SAT. Students frolicked in their high school paradise without knowledge of evil.

But then the Serpent silently slithered into the high school through the hot lunch loading dock. He was the most nefarious, loathsome, malevolent, malicious, odious, insidious, cunning, beguiling, deceitful serpent who ever existed. It was because of this serpent that high school students have to learn vocabulary words like the ones in the previous sentence. This was the Evil Testing Serpent (ETS). The ETS, an unfathomably long, mighty, mucus-encrusted beastie, was determined to bring evil and pain into the paradise. So he devised a plan that would put an end to the happiness of high school students.

This is how his plan worked. For three hours students would have to answer an incessant string of multiple choice questions. The questions would be boring and tricky. Students who gave too many wrong answers would have miserable futures and then die. He called this hideous ordeal the Slimy and Atrocious Torture (SAT).

The ETS inflicted his SAT upon the oppressed masses

of students for many years, and the Serpent's power increased as he drained their meager life forces. Gradually, all resistance was crushed and the tormented youth became accustomed to taking the SAT. Parents and teachers began to view the SAT as a national institution. Long, bleak years of misery appeared to lie ahead for civilization.

Could no one defeat the ETS? Would this merciless serpent continue to strangle its victims into submission? Would Vanna White ever wear Lee Press-On Nails in Glamour Length? Was there no hope for humanity? There was... Three common students, born under the tyranny of the ETS, suffered through the unholy SAT with the rest of their comrades. But afterwards, they made a secret blood-vow to avenge the misery they had suffered at the fangs of the Evil Testing Serpent. They delved into the mysteries of the SAT in the hope of uncovering its weaknesses and defeating it. They soon discovered many ways of psyching out the SAT and outsmarting the ETS. They transcribed their revelations in a stirring document wherein they demonstrated that although the Serpent was mean, their readers would be above the mean. The high school paradise was soon restored and students once again were able to pick freely from the Tree of College. It is that document you now hold in your sweaty, trembling hands.

Here, the cruel tricks of the ETS will be revealed and you will be shown how to use your understanding of the Serpent's methods to your own advantage. Throughout this book, the Serpent will make loathsome appearances and will secrete his foul venom all over the page to protest our revelations of his weaknesses and his trickeries. Soon you will be able to recognize the Serpent's infamous tricks and you will live forever free of the fear of his Slimy and Atrocious Torture.

Buy or borrow *10 SATs* or *10 SATs 2nd Edition* (preferably both). These books are published by the College Entrance Examination Board and contain *real* SATs, not the bogus ones that are in the back of most review books. We recommend that you *do the first test in one of these books before going any further in this book*. Otherwise you won't understand what we are talking about. Also, record your score so that you can see how incredibly your score improves after you've read this book.

We didn't put many practice problems in our book. This *does not* mean that you don't need to practice. It simply means that we couldn't see the point of making up fake SAT questions when there are more than 3,000 real SAT questions in the two editions of *10 SATs*. Other review books contain tons of practice questions, but a lot of the questions are totally unlike the questions that are on the real SAT. Moreover, in many books, several of the given answers are *wrong!* The three of us got so frustrated with the questions in these books that we decided not to make the same mistake ourselves.

In order to use this book effectively

Why doesn't this book have many practice problems?

THE VERBAL SECTION

The verbal section of the SAT tests how skilled you are with words. It tests your vocabulary, your ability to understand the relationships between words, and your ability to read. Basically, though, it's just a glorified vocabulary test.

We have organized our discussion of the verbal section as follows:

Mastering the Question Types
Strategies for answering antonym, analogy, sentence completion, and reading comprehension questions

About SAT Words
A brief discussion of the types of vocabulary words that will be on the SAT

Memorizing SAT Words
Some tips about how to memorize vocabulary words

The Word Lists
An extensive list of vocabulary words that are likely to be on the SAT

Supplements to the Verbal Section
Six handy lists of synonyms and a list of words that are easily confused with each other

On every SAT there are 25 antonyms, 20 analogies, 15 sentence completions, and 25 reading comprehension questions for a total of 85 questions. In this chapter we will go over each type of question individually in order to familiarize you with the different question types and then show you some slick tricks.

You are given only 30 minutes each for the two verbal sections. So you figure, "Great, I have almost 45 seconds

MASTERING THE QUESTION TYPES

RULE #1: KNOW YOUR SPEED

per problem." But this can be misleading. You have to subtract about 15 minutes for the amount of time that you spend reading the reading comprehension passages, so you're left with about 32 seconds per problem. Then subtract another minute from the total test time for those moments you spend watching the kid in front of you pick his nose and maybe another half second for the time that you spend picking your own nose. Now you have only 31 seconds per problem. That's just about the necessary amount of time for most people if they work efficiently. If you find yourself finishing ten minutes early, then you're probably working too fast and being careless. If you aren't finishing all the questions before time runs out, you might have to be a little less careful (or skip the last reading comp passage of each section, as described in Strategy #5 of the reading comprehension section in this book). In any case, it's essential that you take enough practice tests to know exactly how fast you should move. Good control of your speed and timing must be second nature to you during the real test.

RULE #2: DO THE SECTIONS IN THE BEST ORDER

All questions are worth the same number of points. Therefore, you want to have done as many problems as possible in the event that you run out of time. Antonyms take the least amount of time. Do them first. Analogies and sentence completion questions take about the same amount of time. Do them second and third. The reading comprehension section takes the longest; do it last. The only exception to this rule would be if you are a real ditz and jumping around confuses you when you fill out the answer sheet.

RULE #3: REALIZE THAT QUESTIONS GET HARDER

The Serpent gets more and more cruel as a sub-section (a set of 15 antonyms, a set of 10 analogies, etc.) progresses. The first question in a sub-section should be easy. The last question in a sub-section should be hard. This is important to remember because if you know that you're going to have to skip some questions, you might as well skip the hard ones at the end of a sub-section.

Another reason why this is important is that it can be used to outsmart the Serpent. We will explain how you can use this principle to find correct answers to questions that you otherwise wouldn't be sure about. See, since the first few questions in a sub-section always are easy, the obvious or most tempting guess is probably correct. The middle questions in a sub-section are a little harder; on these questions the obvious or most tempting guess is sometimes right and sometimes wrong. On the last few questions in a sub-section, the obvious, most tempting guess is probably wrong. This is a *crucial* concept. As we will explain in more depth later, a question is put at the beginning of a sub-section if, in the Serpent's experiments, most students get it correct. It is put at the end if most students get it wrong. The trick is to learn to pick the answer that "most students" would pick on the questions at the beginning of the section, and avoid the answer that "most students" would pick at the end of the section. What we have explained here is just the basics of how to apply this concept. In Section 5 we provide a more advanced explanation with additional useful strategies and tricks.

Remember, questions only get harder within *sub*-sections and not from section to section. So, if you've finished with the analogies and you are moving on to sentence completion, you'll be starting afresh with relatively easy sentence completions.

If you want an in-depth explanation of this rule and its uses, read the book *Cracking the System* by Adam Robinson and John Katzman. They call it the Joe Bloggs principle.

The directions are the same every year. You should not waste any time reading them during the test. Memorize them from your copy of *10 SATs*.

RULE #4: KNOW THE DIRECTIONS

ANTONYMS

Definition: Use of opposites
Number: 25 questions
Priority: Do them first.
Comment: Antonym questions are usually not too tricky if you know the vocabulary.

Antonyms are *words*, so study words. Learn our word lists, read books, read obituaries, read *The Far Side*, read fortune cookies. Soon you'll be considered erudite and you'll be able to go around making abstruse comments.

Antonyms are unique in that they are words with opposite meanings. *Good* and *bad* are antonyms. When you read the test directions for antonyms, pay close attention to two key phrases. The first key phrase is *"nearly* opposite." This means that the correct answer is not necessarily an exact opposite, it just has to be *more* opposite than any of the other choices. Don't get hung up looking for an exact opposite if there isn't one.

The second key phrase is "distinguish fine shades of meaning." This means that there will be a couple of answer choices that are pretty good. You have to determine the "fine shades" that make one of the answer choices better than all the rest. So, *always read all the answer choices.*

If you know what all the words mean and you see the correct answer, then everything is cool. Problems arise, however, when (1) you are using the wrong meaning of a word, or (2) you don't know what the words mean.

You Are Using the Wrong Meaning of the Word

Sometimes you look at a question and, although you know what all the words mean, you don't see the correct answer. This can really piss you off. The Serpent knows this and therefore likes to use words that have more than one meaning—especially if he thinks that you'll know one of the meanings but not the other one.

Take a look at number 7 on page 38 of *10 SATs 1st Edition:*

7. AIR :   (A) conceal   (B) conform
    (C) detain   (D) mislead   (E) satisfy

Now, when you think of the word *air*, you think of the stuff you are breathing right now. So, you ask yourself, "What is the opposite of air?" It's a dumb question. There is no opposite of air. That's like asking what the opposite of "Velcro" is. People, places, and objects don't generally have antonyms.

But, wait! Perhaps the *air* in this problem doesn't refer to the stuff you breathe. Perhaps the Serpent is using the definition of air that means "to publicize, to speak up," as in "He aired his grievances." Now the correct choice is clearly (A) because concealing something would be the opposite of publicizing it. An aid in dealing with this type of problem is that the answer choices will *always* be the *same part of speech* as the capitalized words. Since in the above example all of the answer choices are verbs, you know that *air* must be a verb, too.

You can answer many of the antonym questions correctly even if you don't know what the capitalized word means or what some of the answer choices mean by using the following four rules.

Sometimes, answer choices for a question have more than one word in them. For example:

1. GIGANTIC :   (A) slightly chubby
    (B) extremely small   (C) totally boring
    (D) hungry   (E) sleazy

Choices (A), (B), and (C) each have more than one word in them. Therefore, if you have to guess, go with (A), (B), or (C). This works because the Serpent *rarely uses multi-word answer choices just for the heck of it when he is making up wrong answers.* However, the Serpent also likes to have *wrong* answers that look as much as possible like the *right* answers.

YOU DON'T KNOW WHAT THE WORD MEANS

RULE #1: IF YOU HAVE A CHOICE, DON'T PICK ONE-WORD ANSWERS

So, whenever he needs to use a multi-word definition to make the right answer, he puts in similar looking answer choices for the wrong answer. You can eliminate some of those wrong answers by following the rest of the rules.

RULE #2: DON'T CHOOSE BOGUS ANSWERS

Sometimes the Serpent puts in an answer choice that is bogus. These stupid answers come in two forms: (1) Words or expressions that don't have antonyms; (2) Poorly phrased multi-word answers.

Let's look at an example of the first form. Let's say you come to this antonym question of *10 SATs 2nd Edition* on page 135 and you don't know what "astronomical" means:

4. ASTRONOMICAL :   (A) unclouded
    (B) occasional   (C) very small
    (D) outwardly calm
    (E) approximately equal

Choice (E) is bogus. What could possibly be the opposite of approximately equal? Approximately unequal? Think about it. There is no such thing as approximately unequal. Eliminate choice (E).

Then you could use Rule #1 (pick multi-word answers) to eliminate choices (A) and (B). Now you have to choose between (C) and (D). Remembering that this is question number 4 (one of the first few questions in the sub-section) you would select (C). You would select (C) because most of the words you know that contain the root *astro* have to do with very big things, especially big things in outer space (asteroids, astronomy, Astrodome), and therefore "very small" is the most tempting guess. Since this is one of the first few questions in the sub-section, the most tempting guess is probably correct. We found the right answer without needing to know what *astronomical* meant.

For an example of the second form of bogus answer choice look at number 2 on page 46 of *10 SATS 1st Edition:*

2. FRAUDULENT : (A) rather pleasing
   (B) extremely beneficial (C) courteous
   (D) authentic (E) simplified

Now, even if you don't know that *fraudulent* is the antonym of *authentic*, you can still eliminate choice (A).
What's wrong with choice (A)? Well, *rather* is an unnecessary word—there really isn't any difference between *pleasing* and *rather pleasing*. Choice (A) sounds like an answer
choice that·the Serpent made up when he was hung over.
(Note: This question is one of the rare exceptions to
Rule #1.)

  Another example of the second type of bogus question
is on page 75 of *10 SATs 2nd Edition*:

5. KNOTTY : (A) youthful
   (B) newfangled (C) moist
   (D) easy to solve (E) known to be true

Choice (E) is stupid. Why couldn't the Serpent just write
true? We will tell you why—because he wanted to have an
answer choice that looked like the right answer, which is
(D). Without choice (E) being phrased like choice (D),
choice (D) would have stood out like a big zit.

This rule is another application of the idea that questions
at the beginning of a section are easy. If you had to know
a difficult vocabulary word in order to know the correct
answer to a question, that question would be difficult and
the Serpent wouldn't have put it at the beginning of a
sub-section.

  For an example of this rule, see page 83 of *10 SATs 2nd
Edition*:

1. HARMONIOUS : (A) appreciative
   (B) discordant (C) fastidious
   (D) elementary (E) unworthy

This is question 1, so it should be easy. But the word
fastidious is a tough vocabulary word. If you had to know

**RULE #3: AVOID
TOUGH
VOCABULARY
WORDS ON EASY
QUESTIONS**

what *fastidious* meant to know the answer to this question, this would have been a hard question and it wouldn't be the first one in the sub-section. So eliminate choice (C).

RULE #4: DECIDE IF A WORD MEANS SOMETHING GOOD OR SOMETHING BAD

If you know you've seen a word but you can't recall its exact meaning, try to decide if it means something good or something bad. If it means something good then its antonym must mean something bad; if it means something bad, its antonym must mean something good.

For example, suppose you see a problem like:

1. MALEVOLENT :   (A) harmful
    (B) incestuous   (C) fictitious
    (D) amiable   (E) thunderous

and you forget what *malevolent* means. But you don't forget it entirely. You remember that it means something bad. You remember that it was an insult when, back in third grade, someone called you a "stupid, smelly, malevolent noodlebreath." That's all you need to get this one right because choices (A), (B), (C), and (E) also have "bad" meanings so they cannot be antonyms of malevolent. Only *amiable* has good connotations, so you would choose (D).

ANALOGIES

Definition: Comparisons
Number: 20 questions
Priority: Do them second or third.
Comment: Easy if you see the answer right away, confusing if you don't.

The word *analogy* begins with "anal" for a good reason. The format of this type of question is illustrated in the examples below. Your job is to find the pair of words in the answer choices that are related to each other in the same way that the two capitalized words are. Your mind will argue with itself about these questions forever if you let it. Think through each question thoroughly but not repetitiously. Most importantly, read *all* the answer choices— don't just grab the first one that looks good.

If you have trouble reading this type of question because of all those colons, use this simple rule:

Single colon (:) means "is related to"
Double colon (::) means "in the same way that"

So, for example

TUNA FISH : STARKIST ::
(A) peanut butter : Skippy

would be read: Tuna fish "is related to" Starkist "in the same way that" peanut butter "is related to" Skippy.

Words can be related in a whole bunch of ways. Although it would be impossible to list all of the possible relationships, here is a list of some common ones that the Serpent uses in the analogy section:

1. Synonyms (obscenity : profanity)
2. Antonyms (pain : pleasure)
3. A thing and what it's used for (the SAT : torturing students)
4. Cause and effect (*Up Your Score* : a 1600 score)
5. Things that go together (peanut butter : jelly)
6. Type of person and something that person would use (sadist : whip)
7. Type of person and something that person would do (sadist : whip)
8. Relative size (pebble : boulder)
9. Relative degrees of the same thing (happy : ecstatic :: interested : fascinated)
10. Description (school lunch : disgusting)
11. Part and whole (marshmallow surprises : Lucky Charms)

WHAT TO DO WHEN YOU DON'T SEE THE CORRECT ANSWER

Situation #1

You think you know the words, but you don't see the answer.

There is a definite procedure that you should follow when you are in this situation. First, you panic and scream. This will distract the other test takers and make your score look good in comparison. Next, you relax and apply the following two principles:

1. Make a sentence

When you're having trouble, the first thing that you should do is make up a sentence that relates the two capitalized words. For example, on page 36 of *5 SATs*, this question appeared:

> 16.   LUNG : WHALE ::
>   (A) shell : clam   (B) claw : crab
>   (C) gill : fish   (D) fin : shark
>   (E) pearl : oyster

Make up a sentence like, "The lung is the organ that a whale breathes with." Then try that sentence out on all the other pairs of words.

"The *shell* is the organ that a *clam* breathes with." Nope.
"The *claw* is the organ that a *crab* breathes with." Nope.
"The *gill* is the organ that a *fish* breathes with." YEAH!
"The *fin* is the organ that a *shark* breathes with." Nope.
"The *pearl* is the organ that an *oyster* breathes with." Nope.

The answer is (C). Making a sentence forces you to clarify the relationship between the words. Make sure that your sentence is as specific as possible. If the sentence had been simply, "*Lungs* are part of a *whale*," then all of the answer choices except maybe (E) would have worked.

2. Look for other relationships

See if you can dream up another kind of relationship between the two capitalized terms. As the following example from page 30 of *5 SATs* illustrates, two words can be related to each other in more than one way.

    42.   COMPLEX : BUILDING ::
        (A) tapestry : fabric   (B) apple : tree
        (C) classroom : campus
        (D) federation : state   (E) highway : truck

If this problem seems *complex* to you, it is probably because you assumed that *complex* meant complicated. However, the definition of *complex* used here is the one that means, "a group of buildings," as in "apartment *complex*." Therefore, the sentence that connects them is: "A *complex* is a group of *buildings*." The best answer, therefore, is (D) because a *federation* is a group of *states*.

If you can't find a relationship between the two capitalized words other than the one you first thought of, try working backwards. Find the relationships between the words in each of the answer choices and then see if any of those relationships work for the capitalized words.

Just as with antonym questions, the parts of speech in the capitalized words will always be the same as the parts of speech in the answer choices. If the capitalized words are "VERB : NOUN," then all of the answer choices will be "verb : noun." So, in the example above you would have known that *complex* was a noun because *tapestry, apple, classroom, federation,* and *highway* are all nouns.

Situation #2
You don't know one or both of the capitalized words.

There is a definite procedure that you should follow in this situation. First, you panic and scream. Scream even louder than you did in situation #1 because you're in more trouble. Then look at the list of choices and eliminate any answer choice in which the two words are not related in a logical and definite manner. This means that each answer choice must get both questions correct on the DOPE.

THE DUMB OR POINTLESS EXAMINATION (DOPE)

Question 1

"Is there a logical and definite relationship between these words that I could make a sentence out of?"

Question 2

"Are they *almost always* related in that way or are they just related in that way in some rare contexts?"

If the answer to Question 1 is "no" or the answer to Question 2 is that the words are *not* "almost always related in that way," then the answer choice fails the DOPE and you should eliminate it.

For example, try this one on page 156 of *10 SATs 2nd Edition*:

42. PHOENIX : IMMORTALITY ::
   (A) unicorn : cowardice
   (B) sphinx : mystery
   (C) salamander : speed
   (D) ogre : wisdom
   (E) chimera : stability

Suppose you don't know that a *phoenix* is a mythical, immortal being. You can still eliminate choice (A) because it fails Question 1 of the DOPE. There really isn't any relationship between *unicorn* and *cowardice*. Unicorns aren't known either for being cowards or for not being cowards. If there's no relationship between two words, they can't be part of an analogy. You can also eliminate (C) because there isn't much of a relationship between *salamander* and *speed*. Salamanders aren't particularly fast; if the Serpent wanted an example of something fast he would have used a cheetah. Salamanders also aren't particularly slow; if the Serpent had wanted an example of something slow he would have picked a snail. Choice (D) can be eliminated in the same way. *Ogres* aren't particularly wise or particularly unwise. If you know that a chimera is a female monster that breathes fire, you can also see that there's no relationship between *chimera* and *stability*. That leaves only

choice (B), which is correct because a *phoenix* is a mythical being that represents *immortality* and a *sphinx* is a mythical being that is famous for posing *mysterious* riddles.

Let's do another. This is number 37 on page 286 of *10 SATs 2nd Edition:*

37. HPARGARAP : SECNETNES ::
    (A) cover : pages   (B) book : chapters
    (C) grammar : errors
    (D) directory : graphs
    (E) summary : comments

You don't know what either of the capitalized words means. But that doesn't matter. You can still eliminate three of the answers because they are dumb or pointless.

Choice (C) does not pass the DOPE. There are such things as grammatical errors but grammar doesn't need to have errors and lots of things can have errors besides grammar. Therefore, choice (C) fails Question 2 of the DOPE. Moving on to choice (D) we see that it fails Question 1 of the DOPE. There is no logical and definite relationship between directories and graphs. Even if you say that some directories have graphs in them, choice (D) still fails Question 2 of the DOPE. Choice (E) fails the DOPE, too. Even if you say that some summaries have comments in them, or that people make comments in a summary, this relationship is not very logical and the two words are not usually related in this manner.

Choice (A) passes the DOPE. There are almost always pages on the inside and a cover on the outside of a book. Choice (B) also passes the DOPE. A book is frequently composed of chapters. We've narrowed it down to (A) or (B). Now you have a 50 percent chance of getting it correct.

By the way, the capitalized words as they appeared on the SAT were actually PARAGRAPH : SENTENCES. We scrambled them. The correct answer is (B). A paragraph is made up of several sentences, just as a *koob* is made up of several *sretpahc*.

SENTENCE COMPLETIONS

Definition: Fill in the blank
Number: 15 questions
Priority: Do them second or third.
Comment: Not that bad once you get the hang of it.

For the sentence completion questions, the ETS presents you with a nice, logical sentence. The trouble is that one or two words are missing from it. Your job is to pick the correct missing word(s) from among five choices. All of the possible answer choices will make sense grammatically, but only one will make sense logically.

Sentence completions are considered by some students to be the hardest part of the verbal section, because they test your sense of "sentence logic" in addition to testing your vocabulary. For example:

> The man was smelly so I plugged my _____.
> (A) ear   (B) toe   (C) eye   (D) socket
> (E) nose

Each of these choices is okay grammatically, but why would you plug your eye, toe, ear, or socket if the man was smelly? You would plug your nose. Usually, the SAT questions are more sophisticated, but the basic idea is the same.

If you approach them properly, the sentence completion questions can be extremely gratifying. When the right words are chosen to go in the blanks, the sentence will have a certain flow, a sort of magical aura that will suffuse your body with a warm, orgasmic glow.

Okay, here are the basic rules.

THE BASIC RULES

There is a basic thought pattern that you should follow whenever you attack a sentence completion question:

1. Read the sentence first, skipping over the blanks, just to get a feel for how the sentence is set up.
2. Read the sentence again, and this time, when you get to the blanks, think of *your own* initial guess as to what

the missing words should be. You may not be able to come up with a specific word, but all you really need to determine is the answer's generic category—whether the word is a "negative" or a "positive" one. When there are two blanks, you should at least decide whether the two missing words are antonyms, synonyms, "good," or "bad."

3. Compare your guesses with the answer choices provided and see if any fit your general idea of what the answer should be.

4. Plug in the answer choice that looks best and see if it makes sense.

5. If it does make sense, then go with it. Otherwise, try all of the other choices and pick the one that works best.

Okay, enough rules. Here are some examples:

1. She insulted Irving's appearance by saying, "Your face is _____."
   (A) cheerful
   (B) beautiful
   (C) handsome
   (D) charming
   (E) a wart-ridden, misshapen mass of
       snotty goo

So it wasn't too tough. Anyway, did you notice that magical feeling when you chose (E)?

Let's try some from real SATs. Here's one from page 27 of *5 SATs:*

19. Until Florence Nightingale made nursing _____, it was considered a _____ profession.
   (A) scientific...painstaking
   (B) essential...dangerous
   (C) noble...lofty
   (D) patriotic...worthy
   (E) respectable...degrading

The way that you should read this question is, "Until Florence Nightingale made nursing *something good,* it was considered a *something bad that's the opposite of whatever's in the first blank* profession." You can eliminate (C) and (D) because *lofty* and *worthy* are both words that mean something good. You can eliminate (A) and (B) because they aren't opposites. Now you know the answer is (E).

Page 101 of *10 SATs 2nd Edition*:

> 18. Although they are _____ by traps, poison, and shotguns, predators _____ to feast on flocks of sheep.
>   (A) lured...refuse
>   (B) destroyed...cease
>   (C) impeded...continue
>   (D) encouraged...attempt
>   (E) harmed...hesitate

The correct answer here is (C). Any time that you see *although,* the sentence will have two parts. The first part will say "blah blah blah." The second part of the sentence will say something that you wouldn't expect considering that "blah blah blah" is true. In the above example, the first part of the sentence says, "Nasty things are trying to stop these predators from munching out." Therefore, you would expect that they would decide not to munch out. However, the *although* indicates that the second part of the sentence will say the opposite of what you expected it to say. So you have to choose an answer that indicates that they are still munching out. The only answer that would fit this idea is (C).

On page 75 of *10 SATs 1st Edition:*

> 17. As a scientist, Leonardo da Vinci was capable of _____, but his mistakes are remarkably few in light of his _____.
>   (A) error...accomplishments

(B) artistry. . . failures

(C) genius. . . works

(D) trivia. . . lapses

(E) innovation. . . achievements

In the same way that *although* was the key word in the last example, *but* is the key word in this example. You should be able to figure out that the two missing words should be in the combination "bad thing". . . "good thing." In other words, you should think to yourself, "As a scientist, Leo made some bad mistakes, *but* his screw-ups seem pretty minor when you look at the good things he did." Scanning down the list of possible answers, you may see that:

(A) is "bad". . . "good"

(B) is "good". . . "bad"

(C) is "good". . . "irrelevant"

(D) is "irrelevant". . . "bad"

(E) is "good". . . "good"

Therefore, the correct answer must be (A).

Other key words that can change the logic of a sentence (like *although* and *but*) are:

despite

except

far from (as in "*Far from* doing blah, blah, the thing has done almost the opposite of blah blah.")

in spite of

nevertheless

unless

while (*While* that is true, it is also true that this is true.)

yet (That is true, *yet* we must also recognize that this is true.)

Note: Using the principle that the questions at the beginning of a section should be easy, you should avoid difficult vocabulary words at the beginning of a sentence completion section. For example, this question is the second one in its section (page 75 of *10 SATs 2nd Edition*):

> 17. Just as congestion plagues every
>   important highway, so it _____ the
>   street of every city.
>   (A) delimits
>   (B) delays
>   (C) clogs
>   (D) obviates
>   (E) destroys

Delimits and *obviates* are difficult vocabulary words. If you had to know the meanings of these two words to get this question correct, then this question would be difficult and it would not be the second problem in the section. So eliminate (A) and (D). The correct answer is (C).

READING COMPRE- HENSION

Definition: Passages followed by questions
Number: 25 questions
Priority: Do these last.
Comment: The first one or two reading comprehension passages should be relatively easy; the last few should be hard. (Note: The questions that follow a particular passage are not arranged from easiest to hardest. However, each consecutive passage is harder than the one before it.)

It is difficult to study for the reading comprehension section of the SAT in any direct sort of way. Indirectly, you can study by improving your ability to read and your ability to comprehend.

We will start with the assumption that you know how to read. If, however, this is not a valid assumption, perhaps the first words that you should learn are *two hundred,* which is short for having to go to college in the Yukon Territory.

The ability to read fast can be a big advantage. So read

only those words that start with *w.* "Hold it," you say, "but then I won't comprehend anything." To which we respond, "Oh yeah, you're right, sorry," and then we suggest, "Try reading everything very carefully and make sure that you comprehend it all." To which you respond, "But then I won't have time to finish the test."

This is the heart-wrenching conflict that you must deal with on the reading comp section: to speed or not to speed. All we can say is, do as many practice tests as you possibly can so that you know how fast you can read and still comprehend as much as possible.

Fancy speed-reading tricks probably won't help much for this kind of reading. Psychologists have found that speed-reading tricks really only teach you how to skim a text by skipping details. On reading comprehension questions you have to know the details.

In order to improve your ability to comprehend, we recommend that you expand your reading horizons. If your reading matter is presently limited to cereal boxes and the phone book, it's time to explore new possibilities. Caution: *Do not attempt to switch cold turkey!* Work up gradually. Many a student has gone into intellectual shock after attempting to jump straight from *Teen Beat* magazine to *The Plasma Physicist's Quarterly.* We suggest that you work up to quality reading material using the following one-week plan:

Day 1: *Tattooed Bikers and Their Ladies* (this is a real mag!)

Day 2: *Teen Beat*

Day 3: *Pro-Wrestling Weekly*

Day 4: *Scholastic Scope*

Day 5: *The National Enquirer*

Day 6: *People*

Day 7: *Soap Opera Digest*

Now you should be ready to tackle the kind of reading that you are likely to find on the SAT. Read things of this kind of quality: *The New York Times, American Heritage, The Atlantic Monthly, National Geographic, Sports Illustrated, The*

New Yorker, Harper's, Vogue, Forbes, and all the back issues of the excellent, but now defunct, *Science 80, 81, 82, 83, 84, 85,* and *86* (available at the public library).

ATTITUDE

"You don't have to watch Dynasty *to have an Attitude."*
— PRINCE

The reading comp section is the one place where you should abandon negative thinking. As impossible as this may sound, it is important to take a positive attitude toward the reading comp section. Why is this? Well, remember the chapter on oral hygiene in the health textbook that you had in sixth grade? No, because it was boring and you didn't *want* to read it. But do you remember the chapter on sex? Yes, because you did want to read it. It's the same way with reading comp passages. You won't remember them if you take the attitude that they are boring and useless. (They are boring and useless, but that's not the point.) Instead, you must convince yourself that you are dying to read them because you are passionately interested in whatever they are about. Get psyched to read them. Treat them as you would a love letter. Treat them as you would a passage from a piece of great literature. Treat them as you would a passage from *Up Your Score.*

There is sound psychological backing for this claim. Scientists have shown that comprehension and retention levels are much higher when people are interested in what they are reading than when people aren't. Your brain just doesn't bother remembering stuff that it knows you aren't interested in.

STRATEGIES FOR THE READING COMP SECTION

The following five strategies can be of help to you when taking the test. You probably shouldn't use all of them because that would take a lot of time. Which strategies you choose is a matter of personal preference. Try them all and see which ones you like.

After you read a paragraph, ask yourself, "Self, what was that paragraph about?" Spend about two to six seconds summarizing the contents of the paragraph to yourself. It helps to look at the paragraph while you are doing this because then you will remember where it was located in the passage. This can save time later when you have to look for the answers. If you are a flake who, like Larry, can read an entire passage before realizing that you weren't paying attention and that you have no idea what it was about, then this strategy might be of help in forcing you to concentrate.

STRATEGY #1

Usually the passage will be composed of some sentences that state the author's main idea and others that contain facts to support the main idea. As you read the passage, underline any sentence that is purely a statement of the author's main idea. It is guaranteed that there will be at least one question relating to these sentences and if you underline them, you won't have to waste time looking for them. We highly recommend that you use this strategy.

STRATEGY #2

You might also want to circle specific facts. However, this can be confusing and time consuming, especially considering that there will probably be only one question that refers to a specific fact.

STRATEGY #3

Skim the questions before reading the passage. This gives you an idea of what to look for while you read. Follow the four guidelines below if you use this method:
a. Only read the questions; don't read the answer choices, too.
b. When you see a question that asks for something general such as, "Which is the best title?" or "The main idea of the passage is. . .," disregard it and go on the next question. Why? Because you should always assume that there will be at least one question like that so you don't even have to bother reading it.

STRATEGY #4

c. As you read the passage, circle anything that is an answer to one of the questions. Don't immediately go and answer the question because that will break your concentration and hurt your comprehension.

d. Make sure that when you read the passage, you don't get so caught up in looking for the answers to the questions that you fail to comprehend the overall meaning.

STRATEGY #5

The Princeton Review suggests that if you are having trouble finishing the verbal sections, you should skip the last reading comprehension passage. They argue that it takes several minutes to do the last reading comprehension section and, since it's the hardest passage, a lot of students get the questions wrong anyway. If you skip it, you will have much more time to devote to the rest of the questions that take less time, are easier, and are worth the same number of points.

THE PASSAGES

There are six reading comprehension passages on the SAT. There are two passages on the 45-question section and four passages on the 40-question section. There will almost always be at least one passage about something scientific, at least one about something historical, one about an art form, one that is an excerpt from a literary work, and one about a minority group.

The Scientific Passage

Do not be intimidated by scientific jargon. The scientific passage will inevitably have some far-out scientific terms that you have never heard of. Don't worry. *You don't need to know scientific terms.* Either the terms will be totally irrelevant or they will be explained in the passage. Take for example the following excerpt from page 111 of *10 SATs 2nd Edition:*

> "...Kinematic studies of such objects show them to be receding from us at a rate proportional to their distance..."

Some students might panic when reading this sentence because of the word *kinematic*. However, there is no need to panic. You *don't have to know* what *kinematic studies* are to answer the questions correctly. You could have answered the questions just as well without the word *kinematic* in the passage.

The second reason why this sentence could be intimidating is that it refers to proportions. Proportions are math and math is intimidating. Once again, there is no need to worry. If you read the sentence that follows the above sentence in the passage you will see that it explains the math so that you don't have to do any thinking:

> "That is, those galaxies most distant from us have larger recessional velocities."

(You don't have to know what a *recessional velocity* is, either.) The expression, "that is,. . ." clues us in to the fact that this sentence is going to explain the previous sentence. You will frequently find this sort of thing in the scientific passages. If you don't understand a sentence, look at the sentences that precede and follow it. Chances are, one of them explains whatever you don't understand.

The Historical Passage

The historical passage will discuss a particular trend or period in history. The author will be making her own interpretations of that trend or period. She will support her interpretation with examples. When the author starts listing examples, read the first example, then skip the rest of the examples and put an "X" (for "X"ample) in the margin near the list of examples. In many cases, the author will also support her interpretations by referring to other historians who agree with her. In other cases, she will refer to other historians who disagree with her so that she can refute their interpretation. Circle the names of historians the author refers to—there will probably be a question about them.

The Art Passage

The art passage will be about literature, painting, sculpture, crafts, music, etc. or a particular artist, musician, craftsman, writer, etc. In *all* of the examples that we looked at, the author had a positive attitude toward the artist or art form. The author might have some specific criticisms but the overall point of the passage will be complimentary. The author will never say, "Beethoven sucks."

The Fiction Passage

The literature passage will be an excerpt from some piece of literary fiction. It is hard to predict what these passages will be like. Don't skim these too quickly. You have to read them carefully so that you pick up the subtleties. However, when you go to answer the questions, do not read too deeply. You might have to interpret the figurative meanings of parts of the passage, but don't try to be profound and read things into the passage that aren't there. Also, make sure that you pay attention to the author's style and tone. There will almost certainly be a question about that.

The Minority Passage

The ETS has been accused of being biased against minorities. In the 1970s, the ETS decided to respond to these accusations by putting a reading passage about minorities on each SAT. This is a pointless political gesture on their part because it doesn't make the SAT any less culturally biased.

As far as we're concerned, the minority passage makes the SAT easier for everyone—minorities and majorities. This is because the ethnic passage is incredibly predictable. You *know* that the ETS is going to say good things about the minority group. That's the whole point of the passage. Therefore, many of the questions are giveaways, for example this one from page 155, *10 SATs 2nd Edition*:

29. The author's attitude toward the Chinese achievements mentioned in lines 1–45 is best described as one of
(A) disbelief   (B) admiration

(C) anxiety   (D) ambivalence
(E) apathy

The only one of these choices that expresses a clearly positive attitude towards Chinese is (B). Of course, (B) is the right answer.

The Evil Testing Serpent is not particularly creative in making up the reading comp section. He uses the same basic questions over and over. The questions fall into four main categories.

THE FOUR TYPES OF QUESTIONS

1. The author is primarily concerned with...
2. Which of the following titles best summarizes the passage?
3. The primary purpose of the passage is to...
4. The passage can best be described as...

Type #1: General (main idea)

1. According to the fourth paragraph, some economists feel that...
2. According to the passage, an atom of which of the following substances will split, releasing energy and more neutrons?
3. According to the passage, Margaret asked Mrs. Horn's opinion because she...

Type #2: Explicit (facts)

1. It can be inferred that the guilds were organized as they were because...
2. It can be inferred that each of the following applies to the *perfecti* except that they...
3. With which of the following statements about marketing would the author most likely agree?

Type #3: Implicit (inferences, reading between the lines)

1. How is the second paragraph related to the first paragraph?
2. Which of the following best describes the development of the passage?
3. The author cites specific examples of the work of slave artisans primarily to...

Type #4: Author's Logic

A note about outside knowledge: Reading comprehension questions refer to what is "stated or implied *in the passage*." You aren't supposed to use any outside information. So if the passage is about the history of celery and you happen to be an expert on that subject, you still have to read the passage. However, the passages almost never contradict accepted outside knowledge. You won't ever see a passage that claims that the earth is flat. So never choose an answer that you know is making a false statement. On the other hand, never assume that you know the right answer just because you know that a statement is true. There might be other true statements among the choices that are more applicable to the passage.

Now it's time to attempt a sample passage. Following the passage are examples of the four types of questions and the answer choices that would follow them.

Modern science has brought us many wonderful inventions — the television, the waterbed, and of course, the aerosol packaging of dairy products. Many more marvelous technological breakthroughs loom on the horizon. The latest development in the field of applied science is no exception. Today, scientists have invented a process through which deceased family pets can be freeze-dried and saved for millennia.

The freeze-dry method will revolutionize family living. When your pet dies, his lovable body will be kept intact. You can keep it on the mantlepiece and take it down to pet it at your leisure — and a dehydrated pet does not require feeding, walking, or litter boxes. The projected uses for freeze-dried pets include gerbil paperweights, goldfish refrigerator magnets, and poodle hood ornaments.

Detractors claim, however, that the dehydration wears off after several years, as moisture from the air enters the animal corpse and causes decomposition. This, it is feared, would attract bacteria into the home. Another flaw in the freeze-drying process is that the pet becomes brittle and breaks easily. For a young child, finding Fido shattered on the living room floor can be extremely traumatic. Finally, it is feared that people who dislike their pets (or even their children) will have them freeze-dried before they actually die.

Although there are problems with the procedure, the concept of freeze-dried pets is a valuable one. If the method is perfected, it will allow a pet to remain an everyday part of the lives of its loved ones and, indeed, it will permit pets to be passed from generation to generation as family heirlooms.

1. This passage is primarily
   (A) a scientific description of the freeze-drying process

    (B) a discussion of the religious and moral questions associated with the freeze-drying process

    (C) a general discussion intended to acquaint the reader with the subject of freeze-drying pets

    (D) an expression of someone's opinion

    (E) an advertisement pushing the freeze-drying process

2. The first paragraph is best described as
    (A) descriptive
    (B) introductory
    (C) irrelevant
    (D) sophomoric
    (E) premature

3. According to the passage one of the specific problems associated with the process is
    (A) a successfully freeze-dried pet attracts viruses
    (B) cost is high
    (C) the lack of qualified individuals to perform the task
    (D) freeze-dried pets are not shatter-proof
    (E) the fear the freeze-dried pets will stick to the wallpaper

4. The author seems to believe that
    (A) freeze-drying is a worthless process when applied to animals
    (B) the difficulties in freeze-drying outweigh the benefits
    (C) it would be easier to freeze-dry an armadillo than a pine cone
    (D) music is the soul against which all pets are hard-boiled
    (E) the goals of freeze-drying are worth striving for

Answers: 1. (C)   2. (B)   3. (D)   4. (E)

Now you have an idea of what reading comprehension

is all about. Most passages won't be that interesting, though. Here's another one:

Eloquence, say many, is the very heart of breeding. When a man comes up to you and says in an intelligent sort of way, "First and former, I would like to explain that I'm as accompliced at speaking as the back of my hand," it is considered rude to glare or give a testy retort. Yet few other options are open to the inarticulate.

An expressive tirade met with a feeble riposte earns the assaulted no points; yet a fluently persuasive and courteous rebuttal will not only gain the advantage but also demonstrate the deep-seated civility inherent in an individual who has been properly brought up.

Unfortunately, however, such subtlety is often lost on the masses. So one could argue that good breeding has little to do with anything, and eloquence should, in light of this, be abandoned.

And yet, there are those of us who abhor in the deepest sense the vulgarity of vocal anarchy, and, clinging to the banner of euphonious evolution, defend unto the oratorical death the right and ability of man to express himself in an accurate and intelligent manner. So, in keeping with this profound belief, it is the pleasure of the well-bred to say—in the most respectful and well brought up way imaginable—"Stuff it."

1. What is meant by the word *tirade* in the second paragraph?
   (A) Sword thrust
   (B) Angry speech
   (C) Confusion
   (D) Prayer
   (E) Appeal

2. Which of the following best expresses the *author's* point of view?
   (A) Eloquence is not at the very heart of breeding

(B) Eloquence should be canned

(C) Vocal anarchy should rule communication

(D) Two hard-boiled eggs are better than one

(E) Man should be able to express himself accurately and intelligently

3. The purpose of the quoted sentence, "First and former, I would like to explain that I am as accompliced at speaking as the back of my hand," is to

(A) confuse the electrician

(B) demonstrate the ridiculousness of vocal anarchy

(C) freeze-dry the reader's house pet

(D) provide some humor to contrast with the sharply critical tone of the rest of the passage

(E) give an example of the kind of eloquent language that the author endorses

Answers: 1. (B)   2. (E)   3. (B)

hypogyrrationalrhombocuboids
diffeomorphism
supermartingale
myelomeningocele
dacryocystorhinoscopy

You probably don't know what any of the above words mean. You probably don't care what any of the above words mean. Once you have finished this book, you still won't know what they mean.

The above words may be interesting and useful. But who cares? They were put here simply to intimidate you. They will not be on the SAT. This is because the SAT tests you on the type of words that a college student would be likely to run into. A college student who ran into any of the above words would suffer a concussion.

ABOUT SAT WORDS

Acquiring the Vocabulary That You Need to Rock the Verbal Section

THE TWO TYPES OF WORDS

There is a certain type of word that just *is* an SAT word. It is impossible to define precisely what makes a word an SAT word, but by the time you have finished our word lists you will know what we mean. For the most part, they are words that you look at and say, "Fiddlesticks, I should know what that word means, but I don't. It's right here on the tip of my tongue but I can't quite. . ." Another characteristic of an SAT word is that it isn't particularly controversial. It won't have much to do with sex or violence or religion or anything that could offend someone. Finally, it won't be a word that could be discriminatory because it would only be known by a particular social class—like polo terminology or ethnic foods. In short, SAT words are just difficult, generic words.

Type #1: Normal Words

Words that you would encounter in the course of doing your homework, listening to articulate people, or watching TV.

Example: If you saw the movie *The Wizard of Oz*, you heard the word *pusillanimous*. However, you probably didn't whip out your pocket dictionary and look it up. Now that you are in training for the SAT, you will have to start looking up any and all words that you encounter. In the section on memory we will explain the crucial "Froot Loops" method of memorizing this kind of word.

Type #2: Decodable Words

Unusual words that they don't expect you to know offhand but that you can figure out if you are clever.

Example: the word *decodable* is a decodable word. You could decode it like this:

    "de" = take out; reverse
    "code" = words or symbols with secret meanings
+ "able" = capable of being

---

decodable = capable of being taken out of its secret meaning

When I started studying for the SAT I had a feeble memory. I would spend a lot of time on the word lists, but nothing seemed to sink in. My feeble memory also affected other aspects of life. One day I met this gorgeous girl and she said, as girls are always saying to me, "I have an unquenchable desire for your body. My name is Jenny and my phone number is 867-5309." I went home and I was going to write her name down in my book of women who lust after me, but—I couldn't remember her name or her phone number. I knew it was time to do something about my memory problem.

So I read some stuff about how to improve my memory. Most of what I read sounded extremely dopey, but I gave it a try anyway. And, as they say in the world of laundry detergent, "It worked! It really worked!"

The moral of my story is that if you have a bad memory, it's not because there is something wrong with your brain, it's just that you haven't learned how to memorize. We will teach you how in this chapter. The techniques we present are more than cute little tricks. They will tremendously improve your ability to remember vocabulary words. You don't have to use them if you don't want to, but if you don't use them, it will take you much, much longer to learn the word lists.

The most important concept in memorizing things like vocabulary words is the *mnemonic device* (nuh-mahn-eck). A mnemonic device is any technique, other than pure repetition, that helps you memorize something. So for each word in the list that you don't know, close your eyes for *12 seconds* and think of a mnemonic device.

Research has demonstrated that the most successful mnemonic devices are visual. If you can associate a word with a picture, you will be more likely to remember the word. For example, if you are trying to memorize the word *opulence* (luxury, great wealth), you should visualize a giant mansion surrounded by manicured lawns and lavish gardens. Above the gold-leaf foyer, the word *opulent* would be spelled out in precious gems. Within, you might im-

MEMORIZING SAT WORDS

Larry's MEMoirs

agine well–groomed fat gentlemen, the word *opulent* stitched in diamonds across their chests, eating huge amounts of caviar molded into the shape of the word *opulent*. If you make your mental pictures extreme in some way they will be more memorable. So make your pictures extremely bizarre, extremely gross, extremely obscene, extremely comical, or extremely whatever you are likely to remember. (Detail is important in mental images like this one. The more details you are able to dream up, the more likely you are to remember the word.)

Move on to the other senses. *Hear* the chorus of castrati in the ballroom singing the word *opulence* over the gentle strains of Chopin played by a 50-piece symphony. *Feel* the silks worn by the ladies and gentlemen sliding through your fingers as you trace the word *opulence* with rosewater over your desktop. *Smell* the delicate and costly perfumes. And of course, *taste* the smooth and exquisitely fine wines enjoyed by *opulent* society.

After you have seen, heard, felt, smelled, and tasted the word you can open your eyes. You're still not done, though. Research has also shown that the more you do with a word, the more likely it will stay in your brain. So first read the word and its definition, then write the word and its definition, then sing the word and its definition, then make up a story about the word, then use the word in a conversation, then tattoo the word and its definition to your elbow, then staple the word and its definition to your goldfish.

Clinical tests have also proven that the pun is a very helpful memory technique. We have used puns to illustrate many of the words in the vocabulary list. (Note: Since we want to make sure that no one misses our subtlety, we have <u>pund</u>erlined each one.)

If none of these techniques works, there is one foolproof method. Neurologists say that if the word and its definition are repeated over and over during sexual activity, they will never be forgotten. There is no scientific explanation for this, but it is a widely accepted fact.

Another phenomenon you should be aware of is the *serial position effect*. Suppose you have a long list of words to memorize and you spend the same amount of time studying each word on the list. According to the serial position effect, you will remember the words at the beginning of the list best, the words at the end of the list next best, and the words in the middle of the list the worst. Therefore, spend the most time on the middle of the list.

Your chances of memorizing something improve if you study it right before you go to bed. While you sleep, your brain sorts out what occurred during the day. The last thought that goes into your brain right before you go to sleep gets special attention while your brain is doing its nightly sorting.

Finally, nobody studies better with music. Experiments have been done with people who swear that they study better with the Screaming Blue Messiahs in the background. But researchers have yet to find anyone who really does.

Two Essential Tools: The Notebook and the Tape Recorder

You must keep a notebook and a tape recorder by your side while you study. When you come to a word that you don't know, you first devote 12 seconds to mnemonic devices, then you write the word, its definition, and a sentence that you make up in the notebook. Keep reviewing your notebook until you know all the words in it.

Do a similar thing with the tape recorder. When you come to a word that you want to remember, record the word, its definition, and either the example sentence that we give you or one that you make up. Then you can listen to the tape while you are in the shower or brushing your teeth. If you can rap or sing some of your words and definitions it's more fun to listen to. If you have a Walkman, you should listen to the tape wherever you go. If your friends ask you what you're listening to, respond casually, "It's 'Gretchen and the Vocab Lists'—they're new out of L.A." If your friends ask to listen, say, "I would, but the record company asked me not to play it for anyone until it's been officially released."

The Froot Loops Technique

Earlier, we talked about the type of SAT words we call "normal." These are words that you've probably encountered but have never bothered to learn. Now that you are becoming an SAT vocabulary expert, you have to start learning these words. Here is our suggested method:

1. Buy a box of Froot Loops.
2. Feed the Froot Loops to your gerbil.
3. Cut the Froot Loops box into 3 × 5 cards.
4. Take one of these 3 × 5 cards with you wherever you go.
5. Whenever you hear a word that you cannot define, write it down on the card.
6. If someone asks you what you are doing, be honest. Say, "I'm writing the word *pusillanimous* on a 3 × 5 card that I cut out of a box of Froot Loops." If the person looks confused, say, "It's okay, I fed the Froot Loops to my gerbil." The person will leave you alone.
7. When you get home, look up the word in the dictionary and write the word, its definition, the context in which you heard or saw it, and an example sentence (which can be the same one in which you initially encountered the word) in your vocabulary notebook.
8. Try to teach the word to your gerbil. He won't learn anything, but it will encourage you to know that you will do better on the SAT than your gerbil.

THE WORD LISTS

Don't be intimidated; there are fewer than 600 words here, and you probably know some of them already. May you be blessed by the almighty vocabulary god until you get to "zyzzyva."

Aa   Aa   Aa   Aa   Aa

aardvark

Aardvark is the first real word in the dictionary, so we figured that we should start with it even though it has never been and probably never will be on the SAT.

abase

lower; humiliate
Bob Uecker is a baseball announcer who is not ashamed to abase himself in Lite Beer commercials.

abash

embarrass
Arthur went to a bash. He drank an excessive amount of alcohol and did some things that he was abashed about the next morning.

abate

to lessen
Abigail's sister screamed, "Ab ate all the cookies!" Later, of course, her anger abated.

abominate

loathe; hate
The terrorist abominated his enemy Nate so much that he put a bomb in Nate's boxer shorts.

absquatulate

to leave; to get up and "squat" somewhere else
This won't be on the SAT because it's mock-Latin slang, but we thought it was a cool word anyway.
"This party's beat, let's absquatulate."

abstruse

profound; difficult to understand; meaningful on an abstract level
Bullwinkle the moose is seldom abstruse.

accentuate

to stress; emphasize
An accent mark accentuates a syllable.
While in New York, it was rude of you to accentuate the fact that Brooklyn people speak with an accent you hate.

acclivity

sharp incline of a hill
A cliff is an example of an acclivity.

a c c l i v i t y

accolade

award; honor
When Mister Rogers received an accolade for being the most boring man alive he was not pleased.
Can you say accolade ? Sure you can.

accost

to approach and speak to
"That snack cost you $3.95!" the salesman said, accosting the customer who didn't pay.

acne

zits

adroit

skillful
R2D2 is an adroit android.

adulate

to flatter and praise so much it's sickening
She adulated him by saying, "I just love the way your eyes match. Where did you get them?"

adulterate

to make impure
If you adulterate your Tylenol with cyanide, it will get rid of your headache permanently.

adumbrate

to foreshadow by disclosing only partially
The economic indicators adumbrated that the price of gas would rise to a dumb rate.

adverse

hostile; opposed; unfavorable (see AVERSE)
"It's tough writing a national anthem during a British attack," complained Francis Scott Key. "The only light you have is the rockets' red glare. You have to add verses under adverse conditions."

advocate

urge; recommend
Advertisements advocate products.

aesthetic

artistic; pertaining to a sense of what is beautiful
As the tick was sucking blood from my arm I squashed it. The dead insect smeared on my arm was not aesthetically pleasing.

affected

fake (Think: a-FAKE-ted)
His affected personality negatively affected our affection.

affinity

attraction
There was a natural affinity between the girl and the dolphin.

affluent

rich
If you are a fluent speaker with a big vocabulary, you have a better chance of becoming affluent.

affray

public brawl
The frog was afraid to enter the affray.

agape

open-mouthed
If you stand agape there is a gap in your mouth.

aghast

horrified
We were aghast when he "passed gas." (see EUPHEMISM. *Passed gas* is an example of a euphemism.)

agile

able to move in a quick and easy fashion
Even though Mary Lou Retton is obnoxious in the Wheaties commercials, she was agile in the Olympics.

alacrity

cheerful promptness
A lack of M&Ms should be remedied with alacrity.

alias

a false name
All I asked for was your name; why did you give me an alias?

alimentary

supplying nourishment
When Watson asked, "What's a ten-letter word meaning 'supplying nourishment'?" Sherlock replied, "Alimentary, my dear Watson."

allay

to soothe; to make more bearable
Note: This is one of a countless number of SAT words that means this. (see ALLEVIATE)
He allayed his parents' fears by getting all As on his report card.

alleged

stated without proof
It was alleged that he died by falling off a ledge.

alleviate

to make more bearable (see APPEASE)
The "Live Aid" concert was organized to alleviate hunger in Africa and to put an end to Ethiopian jokes.

allude

refer indirectly
A lewd person alludes to salacious sexual endeavors. (see SALACIOUS)

allusion

a reference to something
Our "Story of the Evil Testing Serpent" makes allusions to the book of Genesis.

altercation

a violent dispute
An altercation broke out in the church between the altar boys.

amass	collect; get a bunch of By publishing this book, we hope to amass a mass of 1600s for our readers.
ambulatory	able to walk After he was run over by the ambulance, he was no longer ambulatory.
ameliorate	improve a bad situation Amelia rated her relationship as having been ameliorated since last year.
amity	peaceful relations; friendship The root "ami-" means friend as in "amiable." There was amity in Amityville before the horror.
amnesia	loss of memory We forgot our sentence for this word because we have amnesia. (See, after this long wild night of vicious partying, combined with excessive exposure to the sun, and intense snorting of crushed, powdered compact discs, we became so fried that we lost our ability to recall things and to function normally in society, and . . . what word are we on?)
amorphous	shapeless This word is decodable if you know all of the pieces: "a" = not (see ATYPICAL) "morph" = shape, form + "ous" = having the qualities of ___ amorphous = not having the qualities of shape An amorphous cloud of radioactive gas emerged from Chernobyl.
amuck	freaked out and violently pissed off The schmuck in the muck got stuck, ran amuck, and guess what word he screamed? (answer: shucks)

anthropoid

human-like
The root "anthropo-" means human.
C3PO is an anthropoid droid.

antipathy

hatred; aversion; dislike
This word is also decodable:
    "anti" = against
+ "pathy" = feeling

antipathy = feeling against
By this time you should be developing a strong antipathy to studying these words and their ridiculous definitions. Take a break. Put the book down, get a soda, or drink a bottle of cough syrup. Then return to your work, refreshed and ready to continue.

apathetic
apathy

indifferent; showing lack of interest
indifference; lack of interest
    "a" = not
+ "pathy" = feeling

   apathy = not feeling
It's a pathetic thing to be apathetic.
"They found the cure for apathy, but no one showed any interest in it." — George Carlin

apex

tip; peak; summit; way up there
This word is likely to be found in the antonym and analogy sections. Its opposites are words such as nadir and bottom.
At the top of a peak is the apex.

appease

soothe; placate (Think: aPEACE) (see ASSUAGE)
He appeased his parents by eating a piece of slimy okra.

fishhead

the head of a fish
(Just checking to see if you're still awake.)

apt	just right; exactly suitable; apropriate
	The A in SAT stands for aptitude because, supposedly, it's testing how apt you are for scholastic studies. So if this word is on your test, just look at the test booklet cover and you'll have no problem.
	likely
	He is apt to be wrapped in winter woolies.
arbitrary	chosen at random or without apparent reason
	If a college rejects you, its admissions process must be arbitrary.
ardor	heat; passion; zeal
	With ardor she moaned, "You don't have to be so gentle — ardor, ardor."
askew	crooked; off to one side
	Don't tell us our type is askew. Did we ask you?
assuage	to ease; pacify (see APPEASE)
	After the test, try to assuage your hurt and battered egos by tearing the heads off stuffed animals and jamming them onto spikes.
astute	shrewd; wise; observing
	A student must be astute to outwit the Evil Testing Serpent.
atypical	not typical (The prefix "a-" usually means not. For example, amoral means "not moral," asexual means "not sexual," apolitical means "not into politics," and as we have seen, amorphous means "not shaped.")
	Cyndi Lauper's voice and clothing are atypical.
audacity	boldness
	Their audacity was evident when they were unabashed (not + embarrassed) to publish their odd SAT book.

august

majestic; awe-inspiring
Augustus Caesar's palace was august.
I guessed that a gust of wind caused an august wave that made us aghast as it almost crashed down upon our ship last August.

austerity

severity; strictness
His austerity is actually a rarity; severity is not his specialty.

averse

opposed; unwilling
I was averse to writing a verse
So at the teacher I did curse
And put mounds of coleslaw in her purse.
My verse started good but then got worse
As I ran out of things that rhymed with -erse.
Averse is a lot like adverse. It probably wouldn't matter if you got the two confused on the SAT, but for the record, you use averse when you want to say that a person or thing is opposed to something else. For example: Eggbert was averse to eating Frisbees. (Note: To or from always follows averse)
Adverse, on the other hand, is used when you want to say that something else is opposed to a person or thing. For example: Eggbert received adverse criticism for not eating Frisbees; or, Eggbert had to eat the Frisbee under adverse conditions.
In the first example Eggbert is averse to eating, whereas in the second and third examples the criticism and the conditions are adverse to Eggbert.

avuncular

a funky word meaning "like an uncle"
This word does not deserve a sentence because no one that we know has ever used it.

awry

twisted; crooked; out of whack; askew; wrong
"Waiter, there is something awry in my bread," she complained.
"That thing?" He replied, "Why that's just a rye seed."

It is helpful to make up a story using as many of the vocabulary words as possible from the list you have just learned. We have written some sample stories, but you should write your own, too. Here is the first one.

AN ADVEN-TUROUS AARDVARK

The audacious aardvark was rooting around in the grass for some lunch with which to assuage his hunger when his adroit friend Bob the baboon waddled up with alacrity and accosted him. "Hey man," Bob said, beginning an altercation, "Why do you abase yourself in that atypical way? I advocate the agile use of a knife and a fork."

"You are an ass," the aardvark replied politely. "It would be more aesthetically pleasing were I to eat that way, but the use of utensils would be too affected for a simple aardvark such as myself. I am averse to such an idea because it might alleviate my acne, which looks good on me."

"That has to be the apex of stupidity," Bob said, aghast. "Why are you so apathetic about your hygiene? At least you could ameliorate your looks and odor by taking a bath."

"Never allude to my alleged antipathy to cleanliness," the aardvark said with austerity. "Even with your nearly anthropoid form, you still pick lice out of strangers' hair."

Note: The characters in this story are entirely fictitious. Any resemblance to real people, alive or dead, is entirely coincidental.

Bb Bb Bb Bb Bb

bacchanalian
orgiastic; wild drunken revelry
He gave a bacchanalian goodbye party for an alien.

baleful **baneful**	These words are similar in meaning but not entirely synonymous. Baleful refers to something that exerts an evil influence or foreshadows evil. Baneful refers to something that really is poisonous or deadly. (To remember this: baneful rhymes with painful—which deadly things tend to be.) We could see from the proctor's baleful look that he was going to do something baneful to us.
barrister	lawyer When barristers are upset with their clients they throw billiard balls at them. (Well, some barristers do.)
bawdy	obscene; coarse; humorous (see LEWD) Many bawdy jokes have to do with certain parts of the body.
beatific	displaying or producing joy, as in a beatific smile. I feel a strong urge to beat up beatific cartoon characters like The Care Bears.
begrudge	to envy To be holding a grudge for so long against me means that you must begrudge me my happy life.
beguile	trick Don't beguile yourself into thinking that all you need to succeed in life is a box of sardines and a good backhand.
belated	delayed; late We sent a belated birthday present and in return got a month-old piece of ice-cream cake.
bellicose	violent; warlike You'll know you're sitting next to a bellicose person if during the test he stabs his sharpened number 2 pencil into your belly.

benevolent

kind
Superman may be the benevolent protector of the world, but have you ever noticed that he wears his underpants on the outside of his pants?

berate

scold severely
If you don't get into college, your parents will berate you. If you do A work, your teachers won't berate (B-rate) you.

bereft

lacking
The deft pickpocket left us bereft when he committed his theft.

betroth

become engaged
She discovered that he wasn't wearing a tuxedo and that she really was betrothed to a penguin.

biennial

every two years
This word is also decodable:
"bi" = two
+ "ennial" = annual
    biennial = 2 years
My social life has been reduced to biennial parties.

bland

not stimulating; dull
I found the movie about the politics of cauliflower rather bland.

blandishment

flattery
The sycophants obsequiously lavished me with blandishment. (Yes, you should look up each of these words.)

blighted

ruined; destroyed; withered
We were not delighted when we sighted the blighted countryside.

blurt

to say something suddenly and impulsively
The origin of this word is quite interesting. It dates back to the days of William the Conqueror. It seems that William was going to get married to a beautiful woman who was perfect except for one flaw. She had smelly toes. Now William did not know about her toes, but his best friend did. However, his best friend was afraid to tell William. On the day of the wedding, when the minister asked if there were any objections, William's friend stood up and started to blurt out, "Bill, her toes are smelly," but he never finished his sentence, and he spoke so quickly that it sounded like he said Billhert, which has been shortened through the ages to blurt.

bogus

fake (Note: In slang, bogus has come to mean gross, disgusting. This slang meaning will not be on the SAT.) The above story about William the Conqueror is totally bogus.

boisterous

rowdy
We have male cheerleaders at our school. When they get in front of the crowd, those boys stir us up until we're boisterous.

bombastic

grandiloquent (wordy, pompous) in speech or writing
For an example of bombastic writing, see the second example on Eloquence in the reading comprehension section.

braggadocio

cockiness; a braggart
Braggadocios tend to do a lot of empty bragging.

brevity

briefness
Graduation speeches are not known for their brevity. Instead they tend to be bombastic.

brusque

brief; curt; gruff; discourteous
Rambo is brusque with his enemies.

bucolic	pastoral; typical of farms and rural life The scene was bucolic So we started to frolic In our feet so bare, Whoops! The cow chips were there!
bumptious	self-assertive The bumptious people bumped us out of line, so we gave them all fierce head-butts.
burgeon	grow; sprout A great, oozing zit burgeoned on his chin.
burnish	polish One of the housekeeper's jobs was burnishing the furnishings.

It's story time again, boys and girls:

A BOLIVIAN BACCHANAL

They threw us out of the helicopter bereft of any parachute, and the brevity of our flight and brusqueness of our landing were not described in the travel agent's bland brochure.

We found ourselves in a jungle with all sorts of baneful beasties crawling around our feet and baleful animal noises echoing in the blighted jungle.

"Yo," said my bumptious companion with braggadocio as he burnished his machete. "What say we bash our way out of this place?"

But before I could respond, we were captured by a bellicose and boisterous tribe of natives about to perform its belated biennial human sacrifice to the fish goddess. In order to save our skins we had to be betrothed to the chief's daughter Brunnehilde (both of us).

"Yo," said my companion, "This is a bit of a bummer. I should berate you for bombastically beguiling me into going on this vacation."

Then the axe fell and the bacchanalian rituals honoring the benevolent fish goddess began.

Cc   Cc   Cc   Cc   Cc

cache

hiding place (pronounced "kash")
The thieves hid the cash in the cache.

cacophonous

sounding discordant; terrible and generally unpleasant to listen to; the opposite of euphonious
Just because the band's name is Human Sushi doesn't necessarily mean that they will sound cacophonous.
As Dracula arose from his coffin, the wolves let out a cacophonous wail.

cadaver

corpse
The medical students named their cadaver Ernie so that they could be "working in dead Ernest."

cajole

coax
You don't have to cajole Mikey into eating his cereal. He likes it! He likes it!

callous

unfeeling; unsympathetic
Bob complained of his callus on his big toe, but Carol remained callous.

calumniate

to slander (This is one of a bunch of SAT words that mean this—see DENIGRATE)

calumny

slander; defamation (see OPPROBRIUM)
It was calumny when I wrote in *The New York Times* that you enjoy poisoning Arctic wombats. I wrote the column.
I hated you, so I calumniated you.

candor

frankness; candidness
"Speaking with complete candor, Hansel," said the wicked witch, "I have chopped Gretel up and canned her."

cantankerous	ill-natured; quarrelsome "Bloody screaming sea-dogs, I can't anchor us!" the cantankerous captain cried.
capacious	spacious There was nothing in her capacious bedroom but mirrors and a waterbed.
capitulate	to surrender (see RECAPITULATE, which does not mean re-surrender.) Rambo never capitulates.
capricious	impulsive and unpredictable; following whim He just wandered into the auto showroom and capriciously bought a Chevrolet Caprice.
captious	fault-finding "We can't believe you don't know what this word means. Have you no vocabulary whatsoever? Are you brain dead?" the captious review book authors said.
carrion	rotting flesh The lion tore a hefty chunk of flesh out of the zebra's neck. Later the jackals came by and pulled more entrails out of the carrion. After the jackals left, the vultures remained to carry on with devouring it.
castigate	punish Castration is a severe form of castigation.
cathartic	cleansing Manek's method of preparing for the SAT is cathartic.
cauterize	to burn tissue (usually because a scar isn't healing) When the bleeding caught her eyes the doctor knew that she would have to cauterize the patient.

cavil

to raise unnecessary or trivial objections
Someone who is captious will cavil.

caustic

burning; characterized by a bitter wit
When she saw the ugly necklace that her boyfriend bought her, she said to him caustically, "How much did that cost? Ick!"
(Being sarcastic and being caustic often go hand in hand, so relate them in your memory via the non-word sar-caustic.)

celerity

swiftness, speed
When the light turned green the chauffeur floored the gas pedal with celerity and we suddenly accelerated. I nearly spilled my celery tea.

celibate
celibacy

without sex; unmarried
the condition of being celibate
If the prostitute does not sell a bit, she will have to be celibate tonight.
Celibacy is not hereditary.

censor

(v.) to remove inappropriate stuff
(n.) someone who censors things
We hope this book won't get censored by the censors.

censure

criticize; blame
When someone starts to criticize you, you can sense you're being censured.

cerebration

thought (see COGITATION)
The people at the psychologist's celebration were deep in cerebration.

chaos

state of utter confusion
"We don't want to cause chaos," we told the customs official. "So just okay us for passage!"

chaste

pure; unspoiled; virgin-like
The virgin chased away the men so that she could remain chaste.

chagrin

embarrassment
She grinned and blushed with chagrin.

charlatan

quack; someone who pretends he's someone he's not
Charlotte in *Charlotte's Web* was not a charlatan; she really could spell.

chicanery

trickery
When I found the sneezing powder in my Chicken McNuggets, I knew you were up to some chicanery.

chimerical

far out; bizarre; really heady
His dreams were so chimerical that it would take a miracle for them to come true.

choleric

hot-tempered; easily made "hot under the choler"
Mr. T is choleric.

churlish

boorish; rude
Someone who is girlish
Is probably not churlish.

ciliated

having tiny hairs
"Oh Juliet, I love your deep blue eyes."
"Oh Romeo, I love the ciliated lining of your nostrils."

circumspect

prudent; cautious
This is one of those easily decodable words:
    "circum" = around (as in circle)
    + "spect" = look (as in inspect and spectacles)

circumspect = look around (which suggests being cautious).
"Search 'em, inspector," ordered the circumspect detective.

clemency

mildness of temper—especially leniency towards an enemy or in sentencing a criminal
The Mets kidnapped Roger <u>Clemens</u> from the Red Sox, but showed <u>clemency</u> by not executing him.

The following three "cog-" words all have to do with thinking:

cogent

clear; logical; well thought out
The two men (<u>co-gents</u>) on the debate team gave a <u>cogent</u> argument.

cogitate

to think about deeply and carefully (see RUMINATE)
He <u>cogitated</u> about the last question on the test.

cognizant

fully informed and aware; conscious
When the factory repairman becomes <u>cognizant</u> that the <u>cog isn't</u> working, he will fix the gear.

comely

attractive; agreeable (Since we are so tasteful, we won't make the obvious pun. You owe us one.)
Don't be distracted by <u>comely</u> members of the opposite sex during the SAT.

comestible

food
Banana flambé is a <u>combustible</u> <u>comestible</u>.

commensurate

equal; proportionate
You don't think that the two piles of gold are <u>commensurate</u>? Well, <u>come measure it</u>.

commiserate

be miserable together
Decode:

$$\begin{array}{l} \text{"co"} = \text{together} \\ + \text{"miserate"} = \text{be miserable} \\ \hline \end{array}$$

commiserate = be miserable together
He <u>commiserated</u> with his friends who also got 200s.

comport	to behave in a particular way
	The root "port" means carry, as in the words import (carry in), export (carry out), and transport (carry across). In this context, comport has to do with how you carry yourself.
	Comport yourself in a comfortable way.
compunction	strong uneasiness caused by guilt (see REMORSE, CONTRITION)
	I can't see how you sympathize with rebellious people. They're scum! Punks shun society and therefore I feel no compunction about insulting them.
concupiscence	sexual desire; lust; sensuality
	This word probably won't be on the test, but we like it.
concurrent	at the same time
	This is another decodable word:
	"con" = together (see CONVOKE)
	+ "current" = at this time
	concurrent = at a time together
	It is an amazing coincidence that John Adams's and Thomas Jefferson's deaths were almost concurrent; the day on which they both died was Independence Day, 1826.
congenital	existing at birth
	This is decodable: "con" means together and "genital," well, you figure it out.
	Did you become ugly with age or is it congenital?
conjecture	a statement made without adequate evidence
	"Can Jack surely reach that conclusion?" I asked. "Or is it only a conjecture?"
conjugal	pertaining to marriage
	Unless you can juggle both your careers, you will not have conjugal happiness.

contort

twist; bend
We recommend that you contact your local <u>contortionist</u> in order to learn the skills necessary for sitting in an SAT chair.

contrition

remorse; repentance; guilt and bitter regret felt because of wrongdoing
When we broke his priceless garden gorilla sculpture we were overcome with <u>contrition</u>.

convoke

to call together; to cause to assemble
Decode:
    "con" = together
  + "voc" = call (<u>voice</u>)

convoke = call together
The mayor <u>convokes</u> a town meeting so that the citizens can <u>vocalize</u> their grievances.

corp-

a root meaning body
example: <u>corpse</u> = dead body

corporal

of the body; bodily
If they had whipped Radar on M.A.S.H., it would have been <u>corporal</u> <u>corporal</u> punishment.

corpulent

obese; having a fat body
"The Fridge" Perry is a <u>corpulent</u> athlete.

corroborate

testify in agreement
Do you have any witnesses who can <u>corroborate</u> that this is the restaurant where Bonnie and Clyde (<u>co-robbers</u>) ate?

countermand

cancel a command
Mel has <u>countermanded</u> his order that Alice should always keep the <u>counter manned</u>.

covert

concealed; secret
When the press finds out about the CIA's covert operations, the CIA tries to cover it up.

cower

quiver; shrink from fear
The coward cowered.

crass

uncultured
It is crass
To scratch your ass.

credulity

gullibility
His credulity led him to think that the alibi was credible.
My incredulity led me to think that it was too incredible to believe.

crestfallen

dejected
"I'm sorry I dropped the toothpaste," he said, Crestfallen.

crux

main point; central issue; heart of the matter
The crux of the matter is that your ducks ate the pucks.
Think of crux as an acronym for:
central
reasoning
underlying
xplanation

cull

select; weed out
College admissions officers cull the best applications from the pile.

cupidity

greed; avarice
Cupid acts out of cupidity. He works on commission.

A MYSTERY

It was one of those steamy nights when the sky is lousy with stars. I was quietly cerebrating in the office of the Sure-Lock Homes Locksmith and Detective Agency. Sud-

denly, my cogitations were interrupted by a cacophonous
sound and a cataclysmic vibration that reverberated
through my capacious office. I stepped with circumspec-
tion into the hall because I was afraid someone might be
up to some chicanery. I found a corpulent man lying
contorted at the bottom of the stairs. Blood was gushing
through a wound in his side and I could see the ciliated
lining of his small intestine. I decided to take charge.

I asked with compunction, "Golly, are you okay?"

He replied caustically, "Sure, I'm just swell. And how
was your day?"

"Peachy," I said.

At that he bellowed cholerically, "Can't you see I've been
shot? Did you think this hole in my chest was a congenital
condition? Get me to a hospital with celerity!"

"You don't have to be so captious and so churlish."

"Well, if I don't have this wound cauterized soon, I'll be
a cadaver."

At that moment a comely broad walked into the office.
She was voluptuous and yet seemed chaste. I was over-
come with concupiscent thoughts. I smoothly asked her,
"Ig womble splif?" I have a way with dames.

She pointed at the wounded man and said, "We were in
my apartment; he got up to answer the door, and suddenly I heard a cacophonous sound and a cataclysmic
vibration that must have reverberated in your capacious
office."

Just then my trusty assistant, Watt, came into the office.
He said, extending the phone to me, "My kid wants to
know what sort of tree he should plant in our garden.
What do you think, Sure-Lock?"

"A lemon tree, my dear Watt's son," I said.

Then Watt cowered and said, "What is that?"

"It's a plant with little yellow fruit and . . ."

He interrupted me, "No, that body on the floor."

"Oh golly, I forgot. We should get him to a hospital."

We all lifted the body concurrently and put him in my
car. On the way to the hospital, I became hungry so we

stopped at a grocery store to buy some comestibles.

When we arrived at the hospital, the doctor informed us that the corpulent man was dead.

"Golly, that's too bad," I said with contrition.

Well, it was time for me to get to the bottom of this heinous crime. I asked the dame, "Who was that man?"

"My husband," she replied.

"Were your conjugal relations good?"

"Well, no, in fact we had been celibate for a long time."
"Why?"

"Speaking with candor, I chose to be chaste."

"Is it crass to ask why you chose to be chaste?"

"Because it starts with the letter C."

"Aha! Well, did you kill your husband?"

"How dare you censure me like that. What calumny!"

I repeated, "Did you kill him?"

With chagrin, she broke down. "Well, only a little, but Watt will corroborate that. He cajoled me into it."

"Watt! All the time I thought you were on the side of the law and you were really covertly planning this crime. You charlatan. I will bring you both to justice and I'm sure you will be castigated with a prison sentence commensurate with the seriousness of the crime."

Dd   Dd   Dd   Dd   Dd

dais	a raised platform
	The nervous speaker whispered, "Da is no way I am going up on the dais!"
daunt	to intimidate; frighten
dauntless	bold; unable to be daunted
	The dauntless mouse daunted the lion with his .357 Magnum.

dearth	This word has nothing to do with the word death. It means scarcity. (When there is nothing but d'earth there is a dearth.) (see PAUCITY) In the days of the black plague, a dearth of death did not exist.
debase	sink to a lower status The birds at de base of the statue debased it with excrement.
decoy	a lure or bait De coy duck decoyed himself as a poor decoy so that the other ducks would stay away from him.
defenestration	the act of throwing something out the window It's highly unlikely that this word will be on the SAT, but it's the kind of word everyone should know anyway.
delude	to deceive De lewd dude deluded himself into thinking he was attractive.
demivierge	a person whose sexual activities stop short of intercourse (from the French, "half virgin") (This word won't be on the test but think how it will enrich the rest of your life.)
demur **demure**	to object mildly reserved; modest The demure poodle demurred at the St. Bernard's drooling in public.
deplete	lessen the supply or content of She de-pleated the skirt by ironing it, thus depleting the stock of pleated skirts she owned.

depraved

morally corrupt; debased; perverted
The depraved psychotic spread tomato paste all over the TV screen.

derangement

severe mental disorder; insanity
"Do you really think you can get away with not paying my bill?" the psychiatrist cried. "You must be deranged."

derogate

to detract; to take away
The effect of the spear protruding from Bob's forehead was to derogate from his usually good-looking face.

descry

to discern; to catch sight of something that is difficult to catch sight of
Through the mist they could descry the form of the hungry one-eyed, one-horned flying purple people eater munching on a box of Screaming Yellow Zonkers.

desultory

aimless; disconnected; rambling; haphazard
"That speech was so desultory. I could not follow the logic in what you said," she complained.

deter

prevent or discourage from happening
My 18mm bazooka deters de terrorists from entering my yard. They take a detour around my property.

devoid

completely lacking; void; empty; without
The android was devoid of humor.

dexterous

adroit or skillful in the use of hands or body
Houdini was a dexterous man; he could escape from a straitjacket.

diabolical

fiendish; devilish; nastily scheming
The diabolical demon devised a deadly dungeon.

diaphanous

translucent; gossamer
His diaphanous dinner dress caused much discussion.

dichlorodi-phenyltrichloro-ethane	DDT, a spray used to kill insects This word doesn't deserve a sentence.
discern	to detect by the use of the senses The night watchman <u>dis-earned</u> his pay by not <u>discerning</u> the thieves.
discord	lack of harmony "I won't use <u>dis chord</u>, 'cause it would create <u>discord</u>," said Mozart.
disparage	to belittle; reduce in esteem "<u>Dis porage</u> is too hot," Goldilocks <u>disparaged</u>.
disseminate	to dispense objects such as newspapers, etc. While making his stock boy walk the plank, the captain explained, "<u>Dis seaman ate</u> all of the supplies that he was supposed to <u>disseminate</u>."
distraught	anxious; worried; <u>distressed</u> "Why so <u>distraught</u>?" he asked. "My doctor says it's too much caffeine," she answered. "Try <u>dis draught</u> of beer. You'll feel much better."
divers **diverse**	several distinct; varied; differing William Shakespeare's <u>divers verses</u> were about <u>diverse</u> subjects.
doleful	sad; mournful You will be <u>Dole-full</u> and sick if you eat 98 cans of pine-apple chunks.
drastic	severe If your swimsuit strap breaks, you are in <u>drastic</u> need of <u>elastic</u>.

dynamic

energetic; vigorous; forceful
The dynamic duo fell into the Joker's dynamite trap.

Again with the stories:

THE DIS-TRAUGHT DOGCATCHER

Dan was distraught. He knew he'd soon have to go up to the dais and declare his candidacy for dogcatcher. He knew he was devoid of charisma and not a dynamic speaker. He wasn't even dexterous at catching canines. Doubtless, he would debase himself by speaking like a deranged fool.

Trying to appear dauntless, he shambled forward with a dearth of enthusiasm.

"Ahem," he began, but was deterred from continuing when he descried the diabolical Great Dane that was rapidly depleting his audience by devouring them. Feeling these events might derogate his speech, Dan's thoughts were thrown into sudden discord, and he felt a drastic need to defenestrate himself.

Later that day, a supporter disparaged Dan's speech. "It was rather desultory. Rumors have been disseminated that he is depraved. We'll have trouble deluding the public into believing the contrary."

Ee   Ee   Ee   Ee   Ee

ebullient

bubbly; overflowing with excitement
The chef took a hefty swig of cooking sherry and then ebulliently tossed bouillon cubes into the soup.

edify

enlighten; educate
Ed defied the edict against education by trying to edify his pupils.

educe

elicit
He tried to educe as much information as possible from the suspects before he deduced who the murderer was.

efface

erase; rub out
I feel an uncontrollable desire to efface Strawberry Short-cake's face.

effete

tired; barren; uninspired
By the time the review book authors had finished writing the E word list they were effete. (Their readers had been effete ever since aardvark.)

effigy

dummy (mannequin), usually for symbolic torturing
The E words got together to burn an F in F-igy.

emaciated

excessively thin; weak
In May she ate it, but now it's June and she's still emaciated.

emulate

to imitate closely
A mule ate some hay. When I tried to emulate him I became constipated.

epitaph

memorial text carved on a tombstone
I read the epitaph, "Here lies a politician and an honest man," and wondered how they could fit two people in one grave.

epitome

condensed version
something that is a perfect representative of an entire class of things; embodiment
"You're the absolute epitome of stupidity," she screeched after I spilled baloney dip all over her dress.

equestrian

pertaining to horsemanship; on horseback
The equestrian knights went on a quest.

equipoise equality; balance; equilibrium (This is one of those words that isn't often seen in print but might be on the test anyway because it is highly decodable.)

"equi" = equal
+ "poise" = balance

equipoise = equally balanced
An equipoise of speed and comprehension must be acquired in order to succeed on the reading comprehension section.

equivocal capable of two interpretations; ambiguous
equivocate to beat around the bush; to use equivocal statements on purpose
"A good meal from this cook is a rare treat," is an equivocal statement.
I tried to equivocate, but somehow I could sense that my goldfish knew I planned to make him into a refrigerator magnet.

erode to diminish or destroy by small amounts
When a road erodes, there are potholes all over the place.

erudite scholarly
Erudite people use words like erudite.

eschew avoid
"Eschew!" he sneezed loudly.
"Gesundheit," she replied while ducking to eschew the globules of sneeze juice.

esoteric known only by a few people
Now you are one of the few people who knows this esoteric word.

ethereal not of the material world
The lisping child saw the ethereal ghost and asked, "Ith he real?"

eulogy

praiseful speech at a funeral
After the priest delivered the eulogy, he allowed 20 minutes for rebuttal.

euphemism

nice way of saying something unpleasant
"Moved on to the next world" is a euphemism for "keeled over and bought it" which is a euphemism for died.

exact

On the SAT, the Serpent will use the secondary definition of this word, which is:
to demand
The Stamp Act exacted from the colonists exactly what they could not afford to pay. So they "X'd" the act.

exhume

to remove from a grave; disinter (see POSTHUMOUS)
This is decodable:

     "ex" = out of
+ "humus" = earth, dirt

   exhume = remove from earth
They exhumed the coffin, but there was no cadaver in it.

exigent

urgent; requiring immediate attention
It is exigent that I find a sexy gent to escort me to the prom.
excessively demanding; excessively exacting
I made exigent demands on my fairy godmother to find me a debonair prom date and a diaphanous dress.

ESSAY ON EGGPLANT

I want to know which erudite vegetable maker invented eggplant. If he is dead I will exhume his coffin and efface the epitaph from his tombstone. If he is alive, I will burn him in effigy. Eggplant is the epitome of bad vegetables. I eschew eating it. I would rather become emaciated than

eat eggplants. This is an exacting demand but would someone please tell me, without being esoteric or equivocal,
one good thing about eggplant? It is mushy, it has seeds, it
makes my tongue itch, it has a dopey name, and it tastes
like the droppings which an equestrian forgot to clean up.
I wish all of the soil from the world's eggplant farms would
erode. Oh, and get this, when eggplants fertilize each other
the round ones with lots of seeds are the female ones and
the long, narrow ones are the males. And they do it in public, in front of all the other vegetables. What would happen
if humans emulated this behavior?

The end

Ff   Ff   Ff   Ff   Ff

facet

side or aspect; face of something (esp. faces of gem stones)
"Face it! That facet is flawed!" the jeweler cried.
(The personality of Farrah Fawcett has many facets. She's
more than just a pretty face to me.)

facetious

said in jest
She's so facetious that you should not take what she says
at face value.

fallacious

false; wrong; incorrect
They used to castigate people who made fallacious statements. (Well, that was a long time ago.)

fastidious

careful about details, impossible to satisfy
Don't be too fastidious when blackening the ovals on
the answer sheet of the SAT (see "Little Circles" in Section 6).
squeamish, easily grossed out
I'm not fastidious, but when you eat too fast, hideous
food particles accumulate on your upper lip and it's disgusting.

fatuous

inane; foolish; fatheaded
Eating 30 pounds of chocolate a day is a <u>fatuous</u> idea.

fawning

grovelling; overly admiring
The hunter who killed Bambi's mother should have come back and made a <u>fawning</u> plea for forgiveness.

feasible

workable
"I think it's <u>fee-sible</u> for us to pay for the house," he said.

fecund

fertile
The <u>fecund</u> bagels gave birth to a whole box of Cheerios.

fervor

passion
I will fight a <u>ferocious</u> <u>ferret</u> to prove to you the <u>fervor</u> of my love.

fetid

smelly
I am proud to have <u>fetid</u> <u>feet</u> that smell of <u>feta</u> cheese.

fictitious

false; not genuine
Books of <u>fiction</u> have <u>fictitious</u> plots.

filch

steal
Since they had zilch, they decided to <u>filch</u>.

flagrant

deliberately conspicuous; glaring
In front of the crowd, General Lee <u>flagrantly</u> tried to <u>filet</u> <u>Grant</u> with his sword, but failed.

flaunt

show off something
I <u>flagrantly</u> <u>flaunted</u> my physical <u>flawlessness</u> to my <u>fawn</u>-ing followers.

fluctuation

irregular variation
At the terrifying sight of the nasty analogy question, his heartbeat <u>fluctuated</u> wildly.

foible

weakness
The Weeble's foible was that he fell down.

foment

stir up; agitate; incite (Think: when you stir something up it foams)
If you foment the student body in opposition to the administrators, you could end up with no adults to kick you around.

forbearance

patience
He played dead with forbearance until the four bears got antsy and went away.

formication

"a spontaneous abnormal sensation of ants or other insects running over the skin" —*American Heritage Dictionary*

forte

strong point (Think: forts are strong)
His forte was outrunning peeled grapes in marathons.

frenetic

frenzied; frantic; freaked out
When the pilot and the flight attendants became frenzied, the passengers became frenetic.

froward

stubborn (see OBDURATE)
The froward guardsmen refused to retreat, so the protestors could not move forward.

frugal

sparing in expense; stingy; miserly
They told me that I was frugal
Because I bought a plastic bugle.

fulminate

explode; roar; denounce loudly
After he bombed the SAT, his anger fulminated for a full minute, and he began to fulminate against the ETS.

futile

completely ineffective
The one-armed floor layer felt his work was futile since he could lay only a few tiles a day.

FRED THE THIEF

Freddy had a flagrant foible. He filched fish; sometimes with fervor and sometimes with forbearance, but he never fluctuated from his forte. One day his mother said facetiously,

"Freddy, is it feasible that you'll foment a fetid fulmination of fish odor if you continue to frenetically flaunt your filching habits?"

Froward Freddy frowned. "That is a fatuous as well as fallacious suggestion." Then he uttered the following fastidiously crafted verse. "This facet of my abilities provides fish for our otherwise frugal dinner. You should fawn over me, not call me a sinner."

Gg   Gg   Gg   Gg   Gg

gainsay

deny; say something against what someone else says
He tried to gainsay that he ate all of the Gaines Burgers and didn't leave any for me.

garbled

screwed up
The garbled message read, "Please spurgle iceberg before rocking breakfast."

It's puzzle time: Can you unscramble the following garbled word? debgral

garrulous

very talkative; loquacious
Even the Serpent would scare you less
Than talking to someone garrulous.

genre

category
It was difficult to identify the literary masterwork, "My Love Is Like a Grapefruit," as belonging to any specific genre.

germane

relevant; appropriate
If Jermaine Jackson wants to remain a popular singer, he must make sure his songs are germane.

gesticulation — gesture; signal (Somehow gesticulation seems as though it ought to have obscene connotations, but we would certainly tell you if it did.)
Igor gesticulated for Dick to hurry up and enter the laboratory, saying, "Yes, Dick, you're late for your brain transplant."

gibberish — rapid, incomprehensible, or nonsensical speaking, drivel
Most politicians speak gibberish.

gibe — to heckle or mock; to taunt; to pick on
"Nice jibe," the sailor gibed, after we capsized.

gloaming — twilight
Making out in the gloaming is popular among children who aren't allowed out late.

gossamer — light; delicate or insubstantial
She wore her gossamer gown while they made out in the gloaming.

gourmet — one who appreciates fine food and drink; epicure; connoisseur
"I only eat human flesh," the gore-met bull bellowed.

grandiose — impressive; grand
Abe Lincoln had a grandiose nose.

graphic — vivid
His graphic review of the porn film was censored until there was nothing left of it.

gratuitous — unnecessary or unwarranted
Adding gratuitous sex and violence to this book has been the best thing about writing it.

gregarious — friendly; outgoing; sociable
My horoscope tells me to be a gregarious Aquarius.

grimace

(n.) a twisted facial expression
(v.) to make a twisted facial expression
"Things look grim as long as there's a knife at my throat," the victim thought, grimacing with fear.

grisly

gory
The Care Bears movie doesn't contain any grisly violence. (Get it? Grizzly.)

gruesome

grisly; gory
The Texas Chainsaw Massacre, on the other hand, is a gruesome film.

gruff

rude; rough
He spoke gruffly and roughly.

gullible

believing anything
You don't have to know gullible because they took it out of the dictionary.
If you believe the above sentence, you sure are gullible.

LESSER-KNOWN ADVENTURES OF THE THREE BILLY GOATS GRUFF

The Three Billy Goats Gruff met in the gloaming by the gossamer dew near the bridge.

"I'm really scared of that gruesome troll," Billy Goat #1 said, gesticulating toward the bridge. "He doesn't seem too gregarious."

"Yeah, and I heard his gourmet appetite includes a grisly taste for goat's hooves!" #2 added, gibbering with fear. "I really don't like gratuitous violence."

"Cowards!" #3 gibed. "I don't listen to garbled gibberish that only gullible fools like you would believe. I bet that troll is really a cool guy. Watch me cross that bridge!"

"You have a grandiose opinion of yourself, but you're really pretty dumb. So long, bud," Goat #1 replied with a grimace, anticipating the graphic goat-mutilation horror that soon followed.

Hh Hh Hh Hh Hh

hackneyed

overused; trite
The plot of the movie *Halloween VII* was hackneyed. It was just another horror movie about an axe murderer who hacked knees off.

haggard

unruly; wild; wasted; worn
The country singer Merle Haggard always looks haggard.

hallowed

holy; sacred
I was hanging out in the cemetery, but I didn't know I was on hollowed hallowed ground until I fell in a grave.

harangue

mean, nasty, angry speech (Think: a speech that is so loud it impairs your hearing)
The zookeeper gave us a lengthy harangue about feeding the orangutan.

harbinger

forerunner; something that signals the approach of something; omen
Some words have only one sentence in which they are ever used. The sentence for harbinger is: "The robin is the harbinger of spring."

haughty

proud; vain; arrogant
He thinks he's hot. He shouldn't be so haughty.

hedonism

the philosophy of trying to be happy all the time; a funky state of being in which you do your own thing and don't worry about morality

hedonist

one who follows the philosophy of hedonism
(Compare these words to stoicism and stoic, which are their respective opposites.)
You are being a stoic by studying for the SATs so that you can get into college and spend four years being a hedonist.

heinous

grossly wicked; vile; odious
The scarecrows said, "Putting hay in us was a heinous crime."

hierarchy

social pecking order
Archie Bunker wanted to get a raise, a promotion, and to generally move up in the labor hierarchy at the loading dock. I guess he wanted to be a higher Archie.

hirsute

hairy
He was hirsute in his ape costume, which was really just a hair suit. He borrowed it from his girlfriend Rapunzel; it was her suit.

hoary

grey or white from age; old
When someone who is hirsute gets old he is hairy and hoary.

homily

sermon-like speech
The homely preacher delivered a homily.

homonym

a word that sounds like another word but has a different meaning
The German word *sechs*, meaning "six", is a homonym of the English word *sex*, meaning "sex."

THE HOMILY

The hirsute young priest was preparing his homily, but needed advice from the hoary pastor.

"I gotta give a good talk so I can move up in the church hierarchy," he explained. "Can you help me?"

"Though you speak on hallowed ground," the pastor began, "Don't harangue and be not haughty. Don't forget to condemn heinous hedonism, though. A good public response to your sermon will be a harbinger of your advancement." The priest worked all night, searching for hackneyed expressions and hip homonyms. But when dawn came he just said, "Oh, the heck with it."

Ii   Ii   Ii   Ii   Ii

iconoclast

destroyer of tradition
When Bob Dylan showed up at the Newport Festival with an electric guitar, people called him an iconoclast and booed him off the stage.

ignoble

not noble
The ignoble noble committed a heinous crime.

ignominious
ignominy

characterized by ignominy
dishonor; disgrace
They suffered an ignominious defeat.
He could not endure the ignominy of getting 200s on his SATs.

imbibe
imbue

Two similar words:
drink in; absorb
to make wet; saturate; to inspire
If you imbibe the meanings of all these words you will be imbued with wisdom.

imminent

about to occur; impending (don't confuse with eminent, which means famous)
I'm in entertaining and my next appearance is imminent.

immutable

The best way to learn this word is to learn the root "mut," which means change. Then you can decode immutable to mean "not changeable." You will also figure out that mutable = "changeable," mutation = "a change," and transmute = "to change from one form to another."
"A fat person uses more soap than a skinny person" is one of the immutable laws of physics.

impale

to pierce with a sharp stake or point
Just for fun, we took a spike and impaled some Care Bears on it.

impasse

a dead end
If you are trying to pick up a member of the opposite sex and none of your passes are working, you have reached an impasse.

impassive

passive (No, we don't know the clever wordsmith who is responsible for this.)
"It looks like I've reached an impasse," Joe muttered impassively as he slammed into the brick wall on his skateboard.

impeccable

flawless and faultless; not capable of sin
Woody is not an impeccable woodpecker; he is always getting into trouble.

impending

about to take place (see IMMINENT)
The dwarf cowered behind Snow White, sensing imp·ending doom.

imperious

domineering
The emperor was imperious.

impropriety

not proper; not displaying propriety
When Anne White wore a body-stocking to Wimbledon, she was censured for her impropriety.

Here are three words that are sure to confuse you:

impugn
impunity
impute

to attack as false; criticize
immunity from punishment
to attribute (especially a crime or fault) to another
You will not have impunity if you impugn my character by imputing that I have a poor vocabulary.

incessant	non-stop
	That annoying person drummed his fingers on the desk incessantly.
incite	arouse; instigate
	As soon as Madonna was in sight, the crowd of Wanna Be's was incited to jump up and down.
incognito	in disguise, so as not to be recognized. Remember the root word "cog"? Well, this is another example of it:
	"in" = not
	+"cognito" = known
	incognito = not known
	The president mingled with the people incognito to find out what they really think.
incommodious	lacking space; not commodious
	His apartment was so incommodious, there was no room for a commode.
incontrovertible	indisputable
	There was no controversy. The evidence was incontrovertible and Judge Wapner reached his decision quickly.
incubus	a nightmare; mental burden
	(Incubus has another meaning that should help you remember it but, as a matter of taste, we chose not to include it. That ought to entice you into looking it up.)
	The SAT is an incubus that hovers in the minds of high school students.
indolence	laziness
	If you study with indolence, they will send you a note of condolence with your score report.

indomitable	unconquerable; impossible to dominate He was the best dominoes player around; he was virtually indomitable.
inept	incompetent Although Scooby and Shaggy are both inept, they are always paired together.

Two more words that will confuse you:

ingenious **ingenuous**	original; resourceful showing childlike simplicity; innocent Baby geniuses frequently discover ingenious ideas in ingenuous ways. Remember these words this way: Ingenious has an i, like genius, and it also expresses the main qualities of genius.
insatiable	impossible to satisfy You must develop an insatiable desire to learn more and more vocabulary words.
inscrutable	enigmatic; difficult to understand He could not understand why she wanted to remain chaste. He found her inscrutable.
insensate	unconscious; lacking sensation Apollo Creed lay insensate upon the canvas.
insidious	working or spreading stealthily; sneaking inside to do something bad (Don't confuse with INVIDIOUS.) The Evil Testing Serpent uses insidious techniques to torture students.
insipid	lacking excitement; vapid The insipid innkeeper stayed in, sipped wine, and slept.
intangible	not perceptible to the touch; impalpable You can't touch the tangent of $\pi/2$; it's intangible.

invective

abusive put-down
On *Cheers,* Carla uses inventive invective ("You have a personality you could store meat in," for example) to insult people.

invidious

making people angry; offensive
The critics of MTV were concerned about the invidious images in videos.

irascible

easily provoked; irritable
The irascible rascal threw her eraser.

THREE IRASCIBLE FOOLS

Larry, Manek, and Paul were traveling incognito in the incommodious bus. They had reached an impasse in their indomitable attempts to think of sentences for the Is and were nearly insensate with indolence.

"Hey, Manek. Do you have any ingenious ideas for inscrutable, you inept fool?" Larry inquired.

Manek's face remained impassive. "You know you're just inciting me to anger with your insipid invective. If you continue your invidious behavior, I'll become irascible. I may even be forced to impale you. Have you imbibed my meaning?"

"Are you questioning Larry's integrity by implying that he acted in an ignoble manner?" Paul interjected. "I'm sure he couldn't stand the ignominy. But what, ho! I believe our destination is imminent."

So the bus stopped and they got off, continuing to argue incessantly.

Jj   Jj   Jj   Jj   Jj

jaded

wearied, especially by too much of the good life
They lived out their jaded existence wearing jade jewelry and driving Ferraris.

jingoism — extreme patriotism
Like all of the peace-loving Beatles, Ringo does not believe in jingoism.

These three words all begin with "joc-" and they all mean about the same thing:

jocose — merry; joking
jocular — jolly; joking
jocund — merry; jolly
The jocose jockey was full of jokes.
The jocular journalist joined the joker's club.
The jocund judge joyfully jailed the jolly janitor.

Kk   Kk   Kk   Kk   Kk

ken — range of knowledge
"Ken's ken is limited," Barbie complained.

kiosk — pavilion or small open booth where items are bought or sold
The kiosk in Kiev sold knishes to comrades.

kismet — fate
"Kiss me, baby, it's kismet," slurred the drunk at the singles bar.

knave — a clever bad guy
knavery — dishonest; mischievous dealing
"Can Avery join the navy?"
"Never, he is always up to some kind of knavery."

kleptomaniac — a compulsive stealer
Old kleptomaniacs never die, they just steal away.

CRIME DOESN'T PAY

The jingoist became jaded. He didn't feel as jocose, jocular, or jocund as he once did. Eventually, he turned to knavery, robbing from kiosks. It was kismet that he got caught. It takes small ken to be a kleptomaniac. A lesson for us all.

LI   LI   LI   LI   LI

labyrinth

a complicated maze or winding series of corridors
You'd be amazed at how easily the laboratory rats get lost in the labyrinth.

lacerate

to rip; maul; tear; mutilate; mangle
At our school, although you might be able to jump the fence and skip class, the barbed wire and guard dogs will lacerate your body.

lackadaisical

uncaring; lacking in interest or spirit
The florist exclaimed, "I lack a daisy! Call the flower supplier!" But the lackadaisical stock boy didn't pay any attention.

laconic

not saying much; brief; terse; concise; succinct
This sentence is laconic.
There is a Greek story about the war between Laconia and Athens. The Athenians threatened the Laconians by sending a letter to them that said something like, "If we defeat you we will burn your houses, pillage your villages, maul your women and children, etc. . . ." The Laconians sent back a laconic reply that just said, "If." Cool dudes, huh?

lambaste

to thrash; maul; beat; whip; bludgeon with big things and other fun stuff; to scold sharply; rebuke
"Baste that lamb or I'll lambaste you!" the cook yelled to his assistant.

languid — lacking energy; weak

languish — to lose strength; waste away
(Note: As you will notice, a lot of L words mean either "lazy and lacking energy" or "lusty".)
No doubt, learning all of this language is giving you so much anguish that you're starting to languish.

languor — languidness; sluggishness
I can't lie here in languor any longer.

larceny — stealing
Stealing from the cartoonist who does *The Far Side* is Larsony.

lascivious — lusty; lewd
The lascivious lass lusted after Larry.

lassitude — listlessness; a state of exhaustion or weakness
The ship's crew was in such a state of lassitude that they sailed to the wrong latitude.

latent — potential but not yet displayed
He had a latent talent for playing the harmonica, but he didn't discover it until late in his life.
(Note: *Latent* is often used in the phrase *latent talent,* which is a handy memory aid because the two words have the exact same letters.)

laud — (v.) to praise (Think: "Praise be the Laud!")
(n.) praise

laudatory — (adj.) praiseful
Loud laudatory lauds were sung by the critics. They lauded the film.

lecherous — lewd; lustful; given to sexual activity
The country preacher said to the employees in the whore-

house, "Yer goin' to Hades 'cause you let yer house be used for lecherous activities." They replied, "Don't lecture us."

lenient

not severe; forgiving and merciful in nature
When he stabbed my spleen, he ended up in jail for four years, but I still thought the punishment was too lenient.

lethargy

sluggishness; indifference
Are you overcome by lethargy from all this studying? Well it's time to wake up, so:

STOP STUDYING

1. Go to the nearest store.
2. Buy four cups of coffee and a six pack of Jolt Cola.
3. Rapidly consume everything you just bought.
4. Go back to work (and relax!).

lethal

deadly
The lisping landlord said, "If you don't pay the leath, I'll thtab you with my lethal thord!"

lewd

indecent; obscene
The Quaaludes that he was taking made him behave in a lewd manner.

licentious

immoral; morally wild or sexually unrestrained
"I've got my driver's license," she proudly exclaimed. "Now we can be licentious in the back seat of my car."

lima bean

A food that must be scarce in China because my mother always said, "There are people starving in China and you won't eat your lima beans." "Mom," I responded, "there's no shortage of vegetables that taste like Velcro anywhere in the world."

limacine

pertaining to or resembling a slug (It won't be on the SAT but it's really useful.)

lithe

graceful; supple; limber; moving lightly
"Oh no! I've got head lithe! How dithguthting!" she lisped as she turned her lovely, lithe body to face the mirror.

loathe

hate (The last four letters of loathe can be reorganized to spell hate.)
"Pick up some bread at the store, okay?" she asked.
"Why should I?" he replied. "I loathe loaves!"

lubricious

This word won't be on the SAT, but if it was, what would you guess it means? If you guessed lewd you're correct.
He liked to use lubrication when doing lubricious things.

lucubration

hard, scholarly studying (see COGITATION)
Readers of this book won't have to do any lucubration.

lugubrious

mournful or sad
When Lou the undertaker's friends died, he was too lugubrious to bury them. Finally, they got so tired of waiting to be buried that they came back to life and said, "Lou, go bury us."

AN OPEN AND FRANK NOTE FROM THE AUTHORS

With words in this list like lewd, licentious, lecherous, and above all lubricious, you're probably looking forward to a great story. Well, you won't find one here, but not because we were too lackadaisical or languid. We actually did write a pretty lascivious one, but the publisher loathed it. After she read it, she lithely lambasted us with lethal cans of lima beans, lacerating our upper torsos. When she laconically called us "limacine idiots," we left. And so, in protest, we didn't do an L story. Humblest apologies. We hope you'll be lenient and forgive us.

Mm   Mm   Mm   Mm   Mm

macabre

gross; suggestive of horrible death and decay
You will always find this word on the back covers of worthless horror novels.
"This macabre story is about a psychotic dentist who doesn't stop drilling when he gets to the bottom of a cavity."

magnanimous

noble; generous; forgiving; magnificently kind
The magnanimous king allowed the prisoner to live on one condition: that he take the SAT every day for the rest of his life. The prisoner chose death.

The root "mal" means bad. The next few words all begin with "mal":

malaise

a feeling of illness or depression
When I ate the mayonnaise that had been out of the refrigerator for too long, I had a feeling of malaise that made me lazy.

malediction

a curse
The male chauvinist's remarks earned him a malediction from the feminists.

malevolent

wishing bad to others; malicious (the opposite of benevolent)
All year I am malevolent. But I repent for my life on Lent.

malice
malicious

the desire to do bad to others; spite
having malice
Mel felt malice towards Alice.

malign

say bad things about; slander
My line in the story maligned the wombat poisoner.

malignant

showing great malevolence and maliciousness
In an act of extreme malignancy, the bully was trying to break my leg. Suddenly, the doorbell rang. I said to him, "Get off my leg 'n see who's at the door."

malodorous

smelling bad; having a bad odor
The air in the testing center will be malodorous.

maneuver

a skillful or clever move
The captain used a tricky sailing maneuver to rescue the man overboard. Later, the man thanked him, "Man, you very clever."

maritime

1. near the sea
2. concerned with shipping or navigation
We had a merry time when we vacationed in a maritime resort.

meander

to wander around aimlessly
Me and her meandered down the path.

melancholy

sadness; depression; pensiveness
Because her melon wasn't ripe, Berenice was melancholy. When he finds out that she can't elope, he's going to be melon-choly.

mellifluous

sweet sounding; flowing with honey or sweetness
He was an ardent Louis Armstrong fan. He would go see him perform in the grungiest, most malodorous clubs in town because he could endure the smell if Louis would play his mellifluous trumpet.

mendacious

untruthful; lying
When I was young, my parents told me, "Never be mendacious." I didn't know what that meant so I lied habitually.

mendicant

(n.) a beggar

Men dat can't get jobs must be <u>mendicants</u>.
(adj.) practicing begging
The bum lived a <u>mendicant</u> existence.

meticulous

extremely careful and precise
She was so <u>met(r)iculous</u>, she measured everything in millimeters. She also thought that we should go <u>metric</u> every inch of the way.

miasma

a poisonous atmosphere or cloud (often in swamps)
Deep in the swamp, Eugene cried: "This <u>miasma</u> is bad for <u>my asthma</u>."

minuscule

very tiny
<u>Minuscule</u> students go to <u>mini-schools</u>.

monotonous

always at the same pitch; boring; repetitious
This word is easy if you break it up into its parts:
  "mono" = the same, one
   "tone" = sound
  + "ous" = <u>having the qualities of</u>

 monotonous = having the same sound
The concerto played on the one-keyed piano was <u>monotonous</u>.

moo

the low, deep sound that a cow makes
In a low, deep voice the cow made the sound, "<u>Moo</u>."

mordant

bitingly sarcastic or nasty
She <u>mordantly</u> told him that he needed <u>more dental</u> adhesive.

morose

sullen; depressed
If you love learning vocabulary words, you will be <u>morose</u> when you get to the word overt because after it there are no <u>more Os</u>.

When his Cheerios sank he became <u>morose</u> and wanted <u>more Os</u>.

myriad

many; a lot; a very large amount
<u>Mary had</u> only one little lamb, not <u>myriad</u> lambs.

MANEK'S PROBLEMS

In a small <u>maritime</u> village, there lived a <u>morose</u> review book author named Manek. Most of the citizens were <u>magnanimous</u> to him because he was a <u>mendicant</u> but there was a <u>malevolent</u> gang in town who <u>maliciously</u> <u>maligned</u> him. "Hey, Manek," they would yell. "You're more <u>malodorous</u> than a <u>moo-cow</u>."

   Manek bore the <u>mendacious</u> gang no <u>malice</u>, though he wished he could <u>meander</u> through the town's <u>myriad</u> streets without these <u>monotonous</u> comments. He grew <u>melancholy</u> and suffered from a great <u>malaise</u> as he <u>morosely</u> contemplated his problem.

Nn   Nn   Nn   Nn   Nn

nascent

coming into being; emerging (see RENASCENT)
Your <u>nascent</u> vocabulary will cause <u>an ascent</u> in your verbal score.

nadir

absolutely lowest point (The word *zenith* is the opposite of <u>nadir</u>. If you ever get these two confused, just remember that no one would name their brand of TV "Nadir.")
Ralph <u>Nader</u> said that the Corvair was the <u>nadir</u> of automobile manufacturing.

naive

lacking in worldly wisdom or experience
After God expelled them from Eden, Adam said, "The time is <u>nigh Eve</u>. We can no longer be <u>naive</u>."

nefarious

evil
No fairy is nefarious.

nemesis

a vengeful enemy
In the book of Genesis
The Serpent is Eve's nemesis.

neologism

a newly coined word, phrase, or expression
"neo" = new
+ "logism" = idea, word

neologism = new word
Whoever made up the word neologism created a neologism.

neophyte

a beginner ("neo" = new)
The neophyte boxer was new to fighting.

nexus

the bond or link between things
A nexus is a bond that connects us.

noisome

offensive; disgusting; filthy
My parents get angry when I don't clean my noisome room. It really annoys 'em.

nonchalant

appearing casual; cool; indifferent; chilled out
Until I challenged her to a duel, she was nonchalant.

nonplussed

perplexed; baffled
She had expected to get an A-plus on the test; when she received an A-minus, she was nonplussed.

notorious

famous for something bad; infamous
The nefarious noteperson was notorious for leaving nasty notes on people's doors.

novel _____
new; unusual; different
A few years ago there was no Velcro. Then someone had the novel idea of inventing it.

novice _____
beginner; a person new to something
He was a novice when it came to carpentry—he had no vise.

noxious _____
harmful to health or morals
In industrial cities, the water can be noxious, and the people obnoxious.

nuance _____
a subtle variation in color, meaning, or some other quality
I could tell by the subtle nuance in her voice that my new aunt thought I was being a nuisance.

A VILLAIN'S DEATH

The nefarious villain had reached the nadir of his notorious career. He had run into his nemesis, Nice Ned, the sheriff, after stealing some nugatory cash (he often didn't notice the nuances of forged bills). Now he lay dying from two fatal earlobe wounds near a noisome junkyard in the desert.

Looking back, he recalled his nascent life as an outlaw. He had started as a naive novice in New York, but when the noxious city fumes got to him, he headed west where a novel future awaited him. In later years, no longer a neophyte, his nonchalant attitude had left him nonplussed. Now nearly dead, he wanted to establish a nexus with his lost youth, but it was too late.

Oo   Oo   Oo   Oo   Oo

obdurate _____
hardened against good influence
I can't endure it when you're obdurate.

oblivion

the state of being totally forgotten
Lincoln was a great president. It's doubtful that he will ever fall into Abelivion.

obsequious

fawning; too easily compliant
"Please polish my toenails and peel me some grapes," she said to her obsequious attendants.

obsolete

out of style; outdated
The eight-track tape is virtually obsolete.

obstreperous

unruly; defiant; boisterous
High school librarians always say things like, "Let's keep the noise level to a minimum," "Cut the chatter," and "Don't be obstreperous in the library."

obtrude

to force oneself or one's ideas on others; intrude; to stick out
You gotta be some kinda social slob t' rudely obtrude your opinions on others.

obtuse

You may remember that in math an angle is called obtuse if it is greater than 90 degrees. However, the meaning that would be on the SAT is:
stupid, thick-headed (Think: an obtuse angle is "thick" and so is an obtuse person)
(Note: An acute angle is less than 90 degrees and an acute person is sharp-minded—the opposite of obtuse.)
The obtuse man could not draw an obtuse angle.

occult

pertaining to supernatural phenomena
A cult holds occult rituals.

odious

offensive; hateful
The drug dealer was odious—he was trying to "O.D." us.

officious

obnoxious and pushy in giving opinions
The swimming official yelled to the drowning people,

"You shouldn't swim in the lake!" To which they replied, "Oh, fish us out and don't be officious!"

ogle

to stare at
She took off her goggles
So that she could ogle.

olfactory

pertaining to the sense of smell
The stench of that ol' factory was offensive to the olfactory sense.

omnipotent

all-powerful. This word is totally decodable.
    "omni" = all
 + "potent" = powerful

omnipotent = all-powerful
Lex Luther desires to be the omnipotent ruler of the earth, but Superman always defeats him.

omniscient

all-knowing. Again, this is decodable:
    "omni" = all
 + "scient" = knowledge, knowing

omniscient = all-knowing
He read every issue of Omni science magazine in the hope that he would become omniscient.

onerous

burdensome
Would you honor us by helping us carry this onerous box of lead?

opulent

rich
If you are opulent, you can afford to buy opals.

orifice

a small hole, opening, or vent
"I've had a hard day at the orifice," said the dentist.

oscillate

to swing back and forth
"His behavior oscillated," the babysitter reported.
"He would be docile eight hours and then go crazy!"

ostensible

apparent; seeming (but usually not really)
The ostensible reason for giving the Test of Standard Written English is for placement in college English classes. However, in Section 5 we reveal that it is also used for admissions purposes.

ostentatious

showy; pretentious
The Emerald City is Oz-tentatious.

ostracize

to banish or exclude
The ostracized ostrich stuck its head in the sand.

overt

open and observable, not hidden (see COVERT)
On *The Electric Company,* Letter Man can "leap a capital T in a single bound." Since everyone is watching when he does it, it is an overT activity.

A FAIRY TALE

I went to the king, seeking to marry his daughter, but he was obdurate in his refusal. I was obsequious, but he was an odious and obstreperous man who kicked me out of the opulent palace because I was not pleasing to his olfactory senses. I went away, determined to obtrude my marital aspirations on him by raising an army and assaulting his omnipotent forces. However, my own forces were blown to oblivion.

I then went to see Omniscient Olga, an old one-eyed witch who dealt in the occult. When I arrived at the orifice that led to her cave, she ogled me with her one eye. She advised me to go and be of service to the king, to offer to carry out every onerous task, ostensibly out of the kindness of my heart, but really to penetrate the castle and elope with the princess.

I made my way to the ostentatious royal city. As I overtly approached the gate, however, a guard informed me that I had been ostracized from the kingdom. Heartbroken, I left and went to seek my fortune selling doorknobs to nomads.

Pp Pp Pp Pp Pp

palatable

acceptable to the taste; sufficiently good to be edible
(Think: plate-able)
The cannibal found his pal edible and quite palatable.

palliate

to moderate the severity of
"He looks pale; he ate something poisonous," the doctor
said. "We'll have to palliate the poison with an antidote."

pallid

having an extremely pale complexion
He was so pallid that even his eyes had pale lids.

palpable

capable of being touched or felt (see TANGIBLE); real
Bamm Bamm said, "Would you be my pal, Pebbles?" Then
he pinched her to see if she was palpable.

paragon

a model or example of perfection
If Bruce Lee weren't the paragon of self-defense experts,
he and his friend would have been a pair o'goners.

parch

to make very dry, especially by heating.
I get thirsty just playing board games. My throat sure
parches easy.

pathos

a quality in something that makes you pity it; a feeling of
sympathy or pity (remember "pathy" = feeling)
Feel pathos for me as I wander down this path oh so piti-
ful.

parsimonious

stingy
The man was so parsimonious that he would not share his
persimmon with us.

paucity

smallness in number; scarcity (see DEARTH) (Never name
your pet store "Paw City.")
The poor city has a paucity of rich people.

pedagogue _____   schoolteacher or educator
a boring, dry teacher
Pedagogue is the kind of word a pedagogue would use instead of just saying teacher.

pedant _____   a boring person who knows a lot but has little practical experience; dweeb
The pedagogue was a pedant.

pecuniary _____   relating to money
"I seem to be lacking pecuniary support" is a euphemism for "I'm broke."

pedestrian _____   You already know that this means a person traveling on foot. However, when it's used on the SAT it means: commonplace; ordinary
Compared to driving a Maserati, driving a Chevy is pedestrian.

penchant _____   a strong liking; an inclination
Baseball teams have a penchant for pennants.

pensive _____   engaged in deep, often sad, thought
After much deep, often sad, thought, William Penn decided to call his new state pensive-ania.

(Don't get the next two words confused. They have the same first five letters and they both have to do with money, which you can remember because of the word penny. Their meanings, however, are quite different.)

penurious _____   parsimonious; stingy
Scrooge was penurious.

penury _____   poverty, destitution
Tiny Tim lived a life of penury.
(The way to remember the difference is that penury is a

poor word that doesn't have as many letters as penurious. Penurious is a stingy word with lots of letters but it won't give any of its letters to penury.

perfunctory
done routinely, carelessly, and listlessly
If you are beginning to study in a perfunctory manner, it's time for a break. Put on some funk music and let the music permeate your room. But you can't do that, because you don't know what permeate means, yet. So you better forget the break and continue studying.

permeate
permeable
to spread or flow through
capable of being permeated
Your hair must be permeable to Clairol if you want a perm.

perspicacious
perceptive; understanding
If you look at things from all perspectives, you are perspicacious.

petulant
unreasonably irritable or ill-tempered
That pet you lent me was petulant. I'm giving it back.

philanthropy
improving the world through charity; love of humanity in general
We did not write this book out of a penchant for pecuniary matters, as that would have been parsimonious and penurious of us. Instead, philanthropy was our motive.

pillage
to rob violently
SATilla the Hun pillaged the village.

pithy
laconic; concise and meaningful
Instead of a sentence for this word we're going to tell you a joke that we like even though it won't help you remember what pithy means:

The Norse god Thor decides that he's had enough of whatever it is that Norse gods do, so he packs his thunderbolt into a duffel bag and heads for a night of mortal enjoyment. He meets an obliging woman and, to make a long story mercifully short, winds up in bed. What with being Thor and having funky Thor-like qualities, he has a rather acrobatic evening of thornication.

In the morning, Thor wakes up, stretches, and says to his companion, "Ma'am, I have to make a confession. I am Thor."

And she says, "You're Thor? I'm tho thor I can't even pith."

(As told by Larry's roommate, Andrew M. Michaelson.)

(Note: The root "plac" in the next two words means calm.)

placate
appease; pacify; calm
The directors of *Kate and Allie* placated Jane Curtin by letting her play Kate.

placid
calm; composed; undisturbed
Lake Placid in New York State gets its name from its placid water.

plaintive
sad; melancholy
When she realized that Judge Wapner was going to rule against her, the plaintiff became plaintive.

plethora
superabundance; plenty; excess (opposite of DEARTH)
In case you haven't noticed yet, there is a plethora of terrible puns in this book.

plunder
to rob (usually violently); pillage
SATilla the Hun rode in like thunder to plunder our village. He did not steal my golden apple, though, because I hid the apple under my mattress.

politic

shrewd; clever
A politician must be politic.

posthumous

continuing or done after one's death
    "post" = after
 + "humus" = earth

posthumous = after in earth
Suppose the three of us died of "pun"icillin poisoning.
Our book would have to be published posthumously.

pragmatic

practical
The Craftmatic adjustable bed is pragmatic because it is
pragtically automatic.

precipice

cliff; steep overhang
The precipitation, combined with the ice, was responsible
for his driving off the precipice.

precocious

characterized by unusually early development
The high school basketball coach hoped that there would
be some precocious basketball players in our elementary
school so he pre-coached us.

presage

to give an indication or warning of something that will
happen in the future
    "pre" = before
 + "sage" = a smart person who tells people things

 presage = tell before
At the press conference, the psychic presaged that the
next president of the United States would be against free
speech. Upon hearing that, the press aged with worry.

prevalent

commonly occurring or existing
Before knights were prevalent, the world was in its pre-
valiant period.

prevaricate	a religious rite in which everyone faces Princeton, New Jersey, and bows while reciting the solemn prayer, "I believe in Crystal Light." We prevaricated in the above definition. Prevaricate really means: lie; avoid the truth; equivocate
proboscis	a long, hollow snout The bumblebee's proboscis probed for sweet nectar in the flower.
profuse	abundant; overflowing Our prof used profuse amounts of profane language. Then he got fired.
prolific	producing lots of offspring or fruit; fertile; producing lots of work or results The guy who writes *Cliffs Notes* is pro-Cliff-ic.
proliferate	To increase or spread rapidly The pro-life movement proliferated in the fundamentalist part of the state.
pulverize	to grind to bits If I asked nicely, could I pulverize your gerbil?
pusillanimous	timid; cowardly; woozy The lion in *The Wizard of Oz* was pussyllanimous.
putrid	decomposed; foul-smelling (pukey) P.U.! Try disinfecting this putrid sneaker.
THE PLUMBERS	Jack and Bob walked up to the door and perfunctorily rang the bell. When someone answered, they promptly introduced themselves. "We haven't come to plunder," said Jack.

"And we haven't come to pillage," said Bob.

"We're just two pedestrian plumbers. We've come to fix your john," they both added, smiling.

After rushing immediately to the bathroom, they both pusillanimously turned pallid and swore profusely at the sight of the putrid mess.

"I never had a penchant for plumbing," Bob whined plaintively. "But it's better than living in penury."

"Oh, don't be petulant," Jack responded, placidly starting his work. "Just think of your work as philanthropic. Without plumbers, bad smells would proliferate everywhere."

"Don't placate me. I mean, try to be perspicacious. Plumbing is not the paragon of great jobs." Bob continued, "And we only get paltry pecuniary sums."

Suddenly, a plethora of black goop permeated a crack in a valve and Jack, now very dirty, became pensive.

"You may be right," he said. "Let's go into politics."

So together they pulverized the toilet and left.

Qq   Qq   Qq   Qq   Qq

"The world would be a better place if there were more Q-words." —ANONYMOUS

quagmire

literally: a swamp. However, the definition that would be used on the SAT is: a difficult situation that's hard to get out of. (Note: This definition is a figurative use of the first definition.)

Batman was in a quagmire when the Joker tried to drown him in the quagmire, but he escaped by using the anti-quagmire Bat-spray.

quail	to draw back in fear He quailed when the flock of killer quails flew towards him.
qualm	doubt; uneasiness a sudden pang of sickness or faintness At first Batman was calm, but then he got into a quagmire and had qualms.
quandary	A state of uncertainty; dilemma He was in a quandary about whether to do his laundry.
qualitative **quantitative**	having to do with a quality capable of being expressed as, or having to do with, a number or quantity (Quantitative comparison questions are a part of the math SAT in which you have to decide which of two numbers is bigger.) "I did really swell on my SATs" is a qualitative description of how you did on the SATs. "I got a 790 on my SATs" is a quantitative description of how you did on the SATs.
quarantine	isolate because of a disease The health official decided that the people who were sick weren't enough of a threat to the population to warrant quarantining them.
queasy	nauseated; uneasy. Uneasy and queasy rhyme. So does the following poem: When on the boat it got breezy I began to feel queasy. The guys on *Miami Vice* are sleazy.
querulous	complaining; peevish Andy Rooney is querulous. He whines, "How come they call it Rhode Island if it isn't one?"

quip

a snappy response
(We worked very hard on the following mnemonic device, so you better appreciate it.)
Quip = QUIck + Persiflage
You're thinking: "That sounds logical, but what does *persiflage* mean?" Well, that's the problem with this device. *Persiflage* means "flippant conversation or writing." But you probably don't need to know the word *persiflage* for the test because it's a little too obscure to be an SAT word. However, you do need to know it to remember the word quip. Got it? If that doesn't work, try:
Quip = QUIck + Point (i.e., a quip is a quick and witty point made during a conversation)
I said to him, "Be careful with those detergents." He quipped, "Yeah, I know what you mean. I put some spot remover on my dog the other day and he disappeared." (from comedian Steven Wright)

quixotic

having the same romantic idealism as Don Quixote
(Really, this isn't a pun.)
When Don Quixote believed that he was a great knight who killed dragons and fought for justice, he was being quixotic.

quorum

the minimum number of people that have to be at a meeting in order for the meeting to be official
Before the council can begin the boredom
It's required that they have a quorum.

A QUICK MEETING OF MINDS

"Quorum, quorum, we must have a quorum!" shouted the leader.
  "Why?" asked an idiot. "Qualitatively speaking, it's claustrophobic in here."
  "Ahh, we are indeed in a quagmire. We need a quantitative estimate of how many people are here."
  "Yes, it is a bit of a quandary," spoke another idiot. "I

know, why don't we vote on whether or not to begin the meeting?"

"I have qualms about doing that," said the first idiot.

"Quiet, you idiots!" quoth the leader.

They quailed before his wrath, and both felt a bit queasy.

"Now then," said the leader, "don't be querulous. I have a plan. You may think me somewhat quixotic, but I truly believe that if we burst forth with enough clever quips, we might be recognized as not being quite so stupid as we really are. And with that thought in mind, I'd like to close this meeting of the village idiots."

Rr   Rr   Rr   Rr   Rr

rampage

(n.) a course of wild behavior
The guy who was supposed to bring us a male sheep (ram page) went on a rampage and never came back.
(v.) to move wildly
Grandma said, "No one at gramp's age should rampage."

rampant

unrestrained
He was last seen running rampant through the streets.

rant

rave; speak wildly
My parents always rant and rave when I don't wear socks. So I will buy bright orange socks to appease them.

rapacious

plundering; ravenous; greedy
The rapacious Gargamel attacked the peaceful Smurf village.

rapprochement

reconciliation (Think: re-approachment)
We would like to have a rapprochement between the ostriches and the pineapples. Yet owing to the latter's rapacious behavior it seems impossible.

ratiocination	logical, methodical thinking Through a process of ratiocination, you could have figured this word out because it sounds like rational.
rationalize	to make rational; justify Try to rationalize your SAT score—then peel the skin off of your forehead one layer at a time.
ravage	plunder SATilla the Hun ravaged the countryside.
ravenous	hungry The raven was ravenous.
raze	to tear down; demolish They razed the town and generally raised hell.
realm	kingdom The king promised me half of his realm if I would take his verbal section for him.
recalcitrant	stubborn I adamantly and obdurately refuse to admit that I am recalcitrant.
recapitulate	to repeat, or state again, in a form that is more laconic and much briefer than the manner in which it was initially stated Now we are going to recapitulate the above definition: to repeat concisely Think: When a sportscaster recaps the game, he gives a brief summary of what has happened.
reciprocal	mutual We have a reciprocal agreement not to spit watermelon seeds at each other.

recondite

abstruse; profound
His abstruse reckoning was recondite.

rectify

to correct; set right
At first the opposite sides of the object weren't parallel and the angles weren't ninety degrees, but then we rectified it.

recumbent

lying down
They say a certain incumbent president is frequently recumbent on the job.

redolent

fragrant
My sister's cooking was so redolent of red pepper that I sneezed all over the tablecloth.

redoubtable

frightening
We were faced with the redoubtable prospect of dealing with a horde of angry iguanas bearing swizzle sticks.

redress

correcting an injustice
Anne thought it was wrong to wear a blue dress, so she redressed the situation.

redundant

repetitious; done over and over many times; repeatedly repetitive
The above definition is redundant.

refractory

disobedient; obtuse; perverse
The refractory prism refused to refract the light rays so they sent it back to the factory.

refulgent

shining; radiant
The beatific child's face was refulgent until we told her that all the Care Bears died in a forest fire.

refute

disprove
I can't refute your theory that the earth is shaped like a large cold cut, but I think it's a bunch of baloney.

reiterate

repeat (Note: iterate also means repeat)
I would like to reiterate my accusation—I truly believe that you are a noodle head.

relevant

having significant importance
Peanuts are relevant to our elephant's development.

remorse
remorseless

bitter regret
having no remorse
When the remorseless villain took away our telegraph machine for the second time, we were re-morse-less.

reticent

silent; restrained in behavior
She said to Rhett, "Why are you so reticent?" Rhett did not respond.
"Is it because you didn't get a letter from me?" she asked. He nodded.
"But Rhett, I sent you a postcard."

Retsyn

We're not sure what this is, but there's a glistening drop of it in every little Cert.

renascent

coming into being again (see NASCENT)
During the Renaissance, classical culture was renascent.

rob

filch; pilfer; loot; purloin; peculate
You know that rob means steal, but do you know all the words in the definition? Each is a different kind of stealing. Go filch a dictionary and look up the different connotations of each word.

ruddy

having a healthy, reddish color (ruddy rhymes with bloody)

When you get a facial, the beautician makes your face muddy so that it will be ruddy.

ruminate

to chew cud (This definition won't be on the SAT.)

to think a lot about; cogitate

(Note how the definitions are related. "To think a lot about something" is kind of like "chewing something over in your mind." Also, when cows are chewing their cud, they look like they're thinking.)

The chemist went into the laboratory room 'n' ate cheese balls while ruminating about how protein could be used to get out protein.

A ROMANCE

He was recumbent on his bed, ruminating on his renascent affair with the countess. She had left him—he had been filled with grief—and then she had returned. They had reached a rapprochement and were once again reunited as lovers; he was the happiest man in the realm. Or was he?

There was a rap on the door and the air was suddenly redolent of her perfume. "Darling," she said opening the door, her face refulgent with rapture. He frowned as she kissed him and she laughed. "Really. Don't be such a recalcitrant child. You're being altogether too reticent, darling, and I shan't stand for it. It's reprehensible." She kissed him again.

He remained refractory and refused to smile. She came over and reclined next to him. "I'm sorry I left you. I had to, I needed room." She was recapitulating the explanation she had given when she left. He did not respond.

Suddenly there was an explosion on the street below. The countess strode swiftly to the window and looked out. Riotous sounds reverberated through the air.

"It's the Roman army. They've been threatening to raze the city if they weren't remunerated and now they're on a rampage." A group of soldiers began ramming their battering rams on the front door. "Our only recourse is to run to the roof as rapidly as we can," she ratiocinated. Without waiting to see if he was following, she climbed to the roof and crept over to the neighboring building. He hesitated at the juncture between the buildings, momentarily paralyzed by the redoubtable distance to the ground. Then he leapt across, joining her. They raced over the roofs from house to house, with the rapacious soldiers running rampant through the streets below, ravaging the city. "They'll feel remorseful later," she said breathlessly, "when they'll have to rectify all the damage they're doing."

"Undoubtedly they've rationalized their behavior by saying it was the only route left open for them," he replied.

They rested a moment, trying to recover from the exertion. Their faces were ruddy.

"You're wonderfully quick," he remarked.

"I can't refute that. I'm also ravenous. We'll have to risk a reappearance."

The outskirts of town were quiet. They slipped into a restaurant. They were led to a table and gratefully sat down. They ordered.

"Now listen here," he scolded. "I want to discuss our relationship right now." He sipped his red wine. "I want some assurance that you won't run off again and leave me rueing the day I met you."

"Whatever are you ranting about?" she retorted.

He reiterated his request, becoming riled. She laughed. "Darling, you're being ridiculous as well as redundant. It's such a bore, really. Waiter, there's a drop of Retsyn in my soup. Please be good enough to remove it." She turned to him again, "Dearest, you haven't even the most rudimentary understanding of how I function, do you? I shall leave you remorselessly if I like, but I will give you ample warning."

"Well, I suppose that's the best I can hope for," he sighed, once more reveling in her beauty, rekindling his love for her.

"Yes, and I shall expect reciprocal courtesy from you," she continued. "But relax. I'm here now, and so is the rest of our repast, at last."

Ss   Ss   Ss   Ss   Ss

saga
a long adventure story
The previews for TV miniseries always say things like, "*Shogun* is a powerful and passionate saga."

salacious
lecherous; erotically stimulating
"Ooooo, that's so luscious," she said salaciously.

sanguine
reddish, blood colored
The bull's hopes sank when he saw the sanguine wound in his side.
optimistic; cheerful
"I'm so glad to be an arctic bird," sang Gwen the sanguine penguin.

scanty
insufficient; small (often used in expressions like, "The scantily clad models were displaying the fall line of underwear.")

scrupulous
principled; having ethical values
She made advances towards him, but he scrupulously exclaimed, "Screw? P.U.! Lust is unscrupulous."

scrutiny
inspection; study; careful searching
An inspection of Canadian police is a scrutiny on the Mounties.

sedate	to soothe, calm, or tranquilize
sedative	something, usually a drug, that sedates
	On *General Hospital* they give sedatives to patients who are freaking out. Sedatives are drugs that have a sedative effect.
	(If you're into politics, you may remember that Anwar Sadat tried to sedate tension in the Middle East.)
sedition	conduct or language inciting rebellion against authority
	Karl Marx's publisher was demanding. He rejected Marx's first manuscript of *The Communist Manifesto* saying, "This edition does not contain enough sedition."
sequester	to separate; set apart; isolate
	The jury was sequestered for a semester until they reached a verdict in the case of the missing kumquats.
servile	humbly yielding; submissive
	The servants were vile and servile.
shiftless	lazy; showing lack of motivation; incompetent
	The shiftless secretary couldn't type capital letters. (Get it?)
simultaneous	happening at the same time
	I will now attempt to rub applesauce on my chest while simultaneously drinking Spam through a straw and doing a Latvian folk dance.
sinister	foreboding of evil
	Sinister sisters seldom smile sweetly. (Say this 10 times fast!)
skeptical	doubting; disbelieving
	At first, he was skeptical about whether the Lysol would work. But once he saw what an effective germ-killer it was, he was anti-skeptical.

slothful	indolent; lazy The sloth is a slow-moving mammal that lives in trees in South and Central America. I'm sure that if you were confined to trees and ate only fruits and leaves, you'd be slothful, too.
slovenly	messy; characteristic of a slob My mother is always saying, "Look at the slovenly state of your room!"
somber	dark; dull; gloomy Testing halls tend to be somber places—but most are rodent and pest free!
soporific	sleep-inducing The other SAT books are soporific.
sparse	thinly spread or distributed; not crowded A sparse crowd attended the concert at which Barry Manilow sang his favorite game show theme songs.
stagnant **stagnate**	not moving or flowing; motionless; stationary to be stagnant We watched the stag 'n ate our lunch. The stag never moved. It was stagnant.
static	*Not* the fuzzy white dots that show up on your TV when your antenna screws up and *not* the effect produced when you rub a balloon across your head but rather: having no motion; at rest; stationary The situation was static; it hadn't changed in years.
steadfast	fixed or unchanging No matter how many times we tried to fix the clock it stayed fast. It was steadfast. faithful You must be steadfast on Yom Kippur, so don't eat. Instead, fast.

stinkhorn	Look this word up in an *American Heritage Dictionary New College Edition* (not the second edition). The picture is the most phallic image you will ever see in a venerable reference book.
stolid	showing little emotion or pain; emotionally solid Even though I loved my pet stinkhorn, I tried to be stolid when they stole it.
submission	the act of yielding to the authority of another "Poets, priests and politicians Have words to thank for their positions Words that scream for your submission No one's jamming their transmission" —The Police
submissive	docile; yielding The sailors on the submarine were submissive in the presence of the imperious captain.
subvert	to overthrow or undermine the power of The poet was accused of subversive behavior when he wrote a revolutionary poem.
succulent	juicy; interesting Eve sucked on the succulent forbidden fruit.
summon	to call forth; to call together The king summoned his advisor. When his advisor's footsteps could be heard in the hall, the king's submissive assistant exclaimed, "Someone's comin'."
supercilious	haughty; conceited; disdainful All college students are silly, but Princeton students have a reputation for being supercilious. The supercilious person said, "You are a super silly ass." The conceited paramecium was super-cillious.

superfluous

beyond what's necessary; extra
Superman once flew us home without his cape.
This suggests that his cape is just a superfluous item and not something that he needs in order to fly.

superlative

the most; of the highest order; surpassing all others
We're going to be super late if the car breaks down, and Mom is going to be superlatively pissed off.

surreptitious

done clandestinely or by stealth
Lisa snuck into the woods and tapped the sap syrup-ti-tiously.

sweat gland

a small secretory gland in the skin that excretes water and body salts
Are you awake?

swindle

to cheat or defraud
This airplane doesn't really work, but this wind'll keep it up in the air long enough for me to swindle the customer into buying it.
A dating service for crooks would be called "Swindling Singles."

synthetic

not real; man-made; fabricated
Astronauts eat synthetic brussel sprouts squeezed from tubes that taste sinfully pathetic.

sycophant

a servile person who follows and flatters another person in the hope of winning favor
After the concert, the rock star was surrounded by sycophants. Suddenly he screamed, "I'm sick of fans. You guys are crazy. You're nothing more than a bunch of psy-cho fans."

A SHOCKING TRIAL

My sweat glands were working overtime in the stagnant air of the courtroom as I stolidly continued my unscrupulous questioning of the defendant on trial for sedition. Although he remained steadfast in proclaiming his innocence, the jury was obviously skeptical. Compared to me, the other lawyer was soporific; his scanty arguments were sparsely filled with synthetic-sounding facts and his words stagnated as he spoke. The judge just sat somberly in the shadows. I was confident. All further speech was superfluous. I know you'll think me shiftless, but I thought I could afford to be slothful. So, superciliously I said, "The State rests, your Honor," and the jury was sequestered.

Two hours later the jury was summoned, and I waited, drooling salaciously, expecting the succulent word, "Guilty." So I was superlatively surprised when I heard the word "not" as well. "I've been swindled!" I yelled. Then the bailiff hit me over the head and I submissively accepted a sedative.

Now I cultivate stinkhorns and lead a much quieter life.

Tt　Tt　Tt　Tt　Tt

table

On the SAT they would not use this word to refer to the four-legged household object. Rather, the SAT definition is:
to postpone thinking about; to put off until later
The legislature tabled the amendment that would have made tuna fish illegal.

taciturn

untalkative; uncommunicative
When the Soviet citizen wanted to find out what happened in Chernobyl, he called the Soviet news agency Tass. It turned out that it was taciturn about the disaster.

tact

skill in dealing with people in difficult situations (Think: good social tactics)
When at a funeral, it is not tactful to say, "Damn, she owed me money."

tangible	existing materially; palpable; able to be touched Compare with intangible: Love, fear, and hope are intangible. Raisins, antelopes, and pencils are tangible. Tang orange drink is tangible, but I wouldn't want to touch it.
tedious	boring; tiresome; trivial The other team scored so many touchdowns that it became tedious to watch them TD us.
temerity	recklessness; wild craziness; lack of regard for danger Elliot complained about the temerity of the people who came after his friend from space. He said, "You better stop them or E.T. is going to go home." (Sorry.)
temperance **temperate**	the quality of being temperate showing self-restraint by not doing things to excess; moderate She was temperate: She rarely lost her temper and never ate too much.
tempestuous	stormy; turbulent; like a tempest (violent wind storm) When we lose our tempers, eschew us because we behave tempestuously. (If you forgot what eschew means, we "sugg-eschew" go look it up.)
tenacity	persistence; tending to hold on firmly The devoted students took the tests in *10 SATs* with tenacity.
tenet	a principle or doctrine The Ten Commandments are ten eternal tenets.
tepid	lukewarm; a little warm "It's tepid in this tepee," the chief said as he took off his headdress.

terrestrial

of the earth
When I forget all things terrestrial,
I often gaze celestial.
In other words, when I think of space,
I always fall flat on my face.

terse

concise; free of superfluous words
This is
Terse verse.

thwart

to prevent from taking place; challenge
"We must thwart the wart," the dermatologist decided.

tirade

a long and vehement speech
The dean gave the sorority girls a tirade for responding
to the fraternity's panty raid with a tie raid.

torrid

parched by the sun; hot; burning
I plan to rid myself of this torrid climate by moving to
Novisibirsk, Russia.
passionate
Soap opera previews always talk about "torrid love
affairs."

treachery

betrayal of trust; traitorousness
Few crimes are more heinous than the treachery of my
teacher. He once forced all of the students to eat the
school lunch chicken with brown sauce. One student
started to throw up but I quickly warned her, "Don't retch
or he'll make you eat a double portion."

trepidation

fear; a state of anxiety or fear that makes you tremble
We couldn't think of a good sentence so we made up a
bunch of bogus words:
strepidation—fear of getting a sore throat
tripidation—fear of vacations and falling
trapidation—fear of getting stuck

stripidation—fear of taking your clothes off
troopidation—fear of getting drafted or of watching *Hogan's Heroes*
(This should be enough to remind you that trepidation means fear.)

tribute

a gift of acknowledgment of gratitude or respect
I try, but I just can't seem to give you tribute.

triskaideka-phobia

fear of the number 13
If you have triskaidekaphobia, you'll always leave #13 on the SAT blank. (This word won't be on the test.)

truncate

to shorten by chopping off the end
The elephant truncated his friend when he ate his trunk.

Uu Uu Uu Uu Uu

ubiquitous

being or seeming to be everywhere at the same time; omnipresent
The Serpent is ubiquitous. He tortures students all over the nation at the same time.
Take five of those yellow "Post-It" notes and write ubiquitous on each one. Then stick them all over your house. The stickers will then be ubiquitous.

There are a lot of SAT words that start with "un-." However, since "un-" usually means *not*, most of these words just mean the opposite of what they mean without the "un-." For example:
unabashed = not abashed
However, some "un-" words aren't direct opposites. Others aren't even words without the "un-" (for example, uncle).

unawares

unaware means not aware, but:
by surprise; unexpectedly
We came up behind him unawares and saw him in his underwear.

unassuming

not pretentious; modest
Although they were rich enough to pay off the federal deficit, they were unassuming.

uncouth

crude; unrefined; awkward
The uncouth youth simply spoke the truth.

unruly

difficult to govern; impossible to discipline
They were used to living without rules, so they were un-ruly.

unwitting

unaware, not knowing
The Evil Testing Serpent fiendishly devours unwitting students.

upshot

outcome; result (This word was originally archery termi-nology. The last shot of an archery tournament was called the upshot, and it often determined the result or outcome of the tournament.)
Zeke was hit in the rear by an upshot at the archery tour-nament. The upshot of this was that he had to take the SAT standing up.

usurp

to seize the power or rights from another illegally
You slurped my power away by usurping my position.

usury

the lending of money at outrageously high interest; loan-sharking
You sure reek of dishonesty. You probably practice usury.

TUTU STORY

"Don't be taciturn!" urged the intoxicated sheep. "Look at me—I have great tact, and no one could accuse me of trepidation when it comes to talking. In fact, it's often been said that my verbal temerity pays tribute to my tor-rid soul."

However, the temperate turtle held tenaciously to his

tenets despite the tirade of his tempestuous and drunken companion.

The situation was entirely too tedious for me, so I turned to someone else at my table and asked, "Do you think that Congress will table the discussion about the tuna law?"

There was an almost tangible silence. Then a young man put an ice cube in his tepid Tang and said, "That's a touchy subject here. We're all upset about our senator's treachery in supporting the bill."

We're going to try to thwart him," said the turtle tersely. "If that bill passes, I'll truncate his body by chewing his head off, and the upshot of this will be that I will usurp his power."

His words caught me unawares. The turtle had seemed to me to be polite and unassuming, but instead he was uncouth and unruly.

Vv   Vv   Vv   Vv   Vv

vacillate

to waver from one side to the other; oscillate
The doctor vacillated about what kind of vaccination to give me.

vacuity

emptiness; vacuum
The scientists were amazed by the utter vacuity in the proctor's brain.

vainglorious

vain; boastful
Only people who are vainglorious about their vocabulary would use the word vainglorious instead of simply vain.

valor

courage; bravery
The authors displayed their extraordinary valor when they attacked the Evil Testing Serpent.

vehement

with ardor; energetically or violently forceful
They fed the sedatives to the <u>vehement</u> protesters <u>via</u> <u>mints</u>.

-ver-

The motto of Harvard is "Veritas" and the motto of Yale is "Lux et Veritas." Since these two schools are going to be knocking down your door once you get your 1600, you might as well know that "veritas" means truth. When you see the root "ver" in an SAT word, that word probably has something to do with truth. For example:
veracity—truthfulness; accuracy
verdict—true conclusion
verification—proof that something is true
verisimilar—appearing to be true or possible
verisimilitude—the quality of being verisimilar
veritable—unquestionable; actual; true
verity—a statement or belief considered to be the permanent truth
vermicide—anything used to kill worms (Well, it doesn't always work.)

verbose

excessively wordy
They wrote and transcribed and copied down on to paper and composed and thought of and typed a sentence that would be <u>verbose</u> because it had excessive <u>verbs</u>.

vex
vexation

to irritate or bother
the act of vexing
His <u>vexing</u> habit of reciting vocabulary words during sexual activity ruined his <u>vex</u> life.

vilify

to slander; defame
You will <u>cavil</u> if I <u>vilify</u> you.

(Note: The next two words have the same first six letters. The two words are related, but not at all synonymous.)

vindicate

to clear of blame or suspicion
The lawyers will <u>vindicate</u> their client by displaying evi-

dence that they have indicating that he didn't mean to steal the Spam from the grocery store.

vindictive

vengeful
The vindictive witch wanted to kill Dorothy in order to avenge the death of the Wicked Witch of the East.

vivacious

animated; full of energy
The Viva Italian salad dressing was served by the vivacious host.

vocabulary

what you need to get a good verbal score

vociferous

loud; obnoxious as hell
The vociferous student demanded in a loud voice that the proctor turn on the lights before handing out the tests.

voluble

fluent in speech (esp. in the derogatory sense of someone who talks too much)
The professor was so voluble that we had to take volumes of notes.

vomiturition

forceful attempts at vomiting that don't work
(This won't be on the SAT, but it's a great word anyway.)

voracious

eager to consume mounds of food
We were so voracious that we even ate the Tupperware. Then we engaged in vomiturition.

vulnerable

unprotected
The Evil Testing Serpent is vulnerable to those who know his weaknesses.

Ww   Ww   Ww   Ww   Ww

wanton

immoral; unchaste; cruel
His blowing up the one-ton truck was an act of wanton destruction.
They had a wanton night of passionate entanglement in a vat of won-ton soup.

whim

a capricious, freakish idea
Although he appeared wanton, on a whim she decided to go with him.

wily

crafty
Wile E. Coyote uses wily methods of sneaking up on the Roadrunner while he isn't looking.

wrath

anger; rage
The Grapes of Wrath is a novel by John Steinbeck about the wrath that people felt about having no grapes during the depression.

wistful

yearning; wishful with a hint of sadness
As he thought of his lost love, he whistled a wistful melody and drank a bottle of her perfume.

wow

of or pertaining to golly-gee-whillikers

Sorry, there are no SAT words that begin with X.

Yy   Yy   Yy   Yy   Yy

yummy

delicious
Well, we didn't want to cop out for two letters in a row!

AN AVUNCU-LAR VENDETTA

My uncle was valorous, yet he was inclined to be quite voluble when faced with danger and thus generally avoided confronting his fate since fate usually left before the end of his verbose, vacuous speeches. Certain vindictive individuals have attempted to vilify his reputation by insisting that he was devoid of temerity but he has always managed to vindicate himself by vehemently verifying the veracity of his claims of courage.

Anyway, one day while my uncle was vacillating over a choice of beverages, the vainglorious Victor Ventura burst in on him, extremely vexed. He voiced his message vociferously: "I consider you a vile swine, and in the future I will not hesitate to spray you with vermicide."

"Pray tell," said my uncle vivaciously, "what is the cause of your vexation?"

"I came here with a voracious appetite," replied Victor, "and on a whim you wantonly denied me any food, you wretched worm."

"Wow," said my wily uncle wistfully, "you may as well spare me your wrath, because I haven't got anything yummy to offer you."

Zz Zz Zz Zz Zz

zany

crazy; insane
On the advertisement for *Tom and Jerry* cartoons, the voice says, "Tune in and watch the zany antics of Tom and Jerry every Thursday at 3:30." But you'll be studying at that time.

zeal
zealous

enthusiasm
full of zeal
The zealous seal spun the ball with zeal.

zenith

peak; summit; acme (see NADIR, zenith's antonym)
If the Zenith company could invent a TV that would

change channels automatically whenever a show started getting stupid, that would be the <u>zenith</u> of television technology.

zest

gusto; happy and vivacious enjoyment
If you use <u>Zest</u> soap, you will feel full of <u>zest</u> for the rest of the day.

zyzzyva

any of various tropical weevils of the genus <u>Zyzzyva</u>, often destructive to plants
Who cares about <u>zyzzyvas</u>? You are done with the word lists. Congratulations! Think of all the words you know now that you didn't used to know. Good work. You are going to rock on the verbal section.

A FINAL POEM

A <u>zany</u>, <u>zealous</u>
<u>Zyzzyva</u>
<u>Zestfully</u>
Climbed to the
<u>Zenith</u>.

SUPPLEMENTS TO THE VERBAL SECTION

A. The following are lists of synonymous SAT words. Actually, they aren't exact synonyms, but they are closely related. When one of these words shows up on the test, it is usually enough to recognize that it's one of the *slander* words, for example. However, sometimes you have to know the word's specific connotations. Use these lists only as aids; you should know the particular meanings of each word.

Stealing/Plunder	Wealth	Slander
larceny	opulence	calumniate
plunder	superfluity	vilify
filching	ostentation	make innuendo
depredation	affluence	insinuate
kleptomania		denigrate
pillage		be captious
swindle		malign
ravage		
rob		
loot		
pilfer		
purloin		
peculate		
filch		

Stingy/Greedy	Soothe/Make Better	Brief/To the point
penurious	assuage	laconic
parsimonious	alleviate	brevity
avaricious	appease	terse
frugal	ameliorate	pithy
cupidity	sedate	
	allay	
	mollify	
	mitigate	
	palliate	

B. The following is a list of pairs of words that look similar and are easily confused with each other.
1. adulate and adulterate
2. adverse and averse
3. anachronism and anarchism
4. antipathy and apathy
5. ascetic and aesthetic

6. baleful and baneful
7. censure and censor
8. capitulate and recapitulate
9. disparate and desperate
10. divers and diverse
11. elicit and illicit
12. heterogeneous and homogeneous
13. illusion and allusion
14. imbibe and imbue
15. imminent and eminent
16. mendicant and mendacious
17. penury and penurious
18. pestilence and petulance
19. qualitative and quantitative
20. zyzzyva and aardvark

THE MATH SECTION

As most people know, the most appropriate place for doing math is in the bathroom. First of all, there are many geometric shapes in the bathroom: square tiles, round drains, cylindrical toilet paper rolls. Second, there is generally ample time for even the most freakish discoveries—an ancient Greek calculated π to 70 digits while relaxing on a pay toilet in fourth-century Ithaca. Einstein himself concluded that space is bent while trying to catch a slippery bar of soap during an excursion in the tub.

What we mean to say is that when you go to the bathroom, you're not doing anything else useful, so you might as well study math.

The material in this chapter can be studied while you are in the bathroom. That way you'll be making efficient use of your time and your knowledge of math will be strengthened.

This was Larry's idea, by the way.

The chapter is organized into seven main categories—arithmetic, fractions/units, word problems, equations, geometry problems, quantitative comparisons, and funny symbol questions. We do not intend to teach you the fundamentals of mathematics—instead we're showing you test-wise problem-solving techniques. If you have trouble with very basic things, then you ought to talk to your math teacher: Direct contact with a good teacher is far more useful than anything we could tell you.

Sometimes in this chapter, we will discuss some relatively advanced subjects. If you are shooting for a math score of above 550, we recommend that you learn the material in these sections. The advanced sections will be indicated by gray bars. Even if you are not a math guru, you should still read the advanced sections. If you can follow what's going on in the advanced part, great. Otherwise, if you're not shooting for a great math score, don't worry about it.

Quick and accurate are the operational words for the

THEORY OF STUDY

math section. If you run out of time, you lose points. And if you do things wrong, you lose points. Either way, your grandmother won't be able to brag about your scores (and you wouldn't want that, would you?).

Arithmetic

1. Know how to multiply quickly in your head.

There are some tricks you can use. You probably use them already but may not realize it. Knowing them consciously will help.

a. DISTRIBUTIVE LAW

20×23 Can you do this in your head quickly?
$= 20 \times (20 + 3)$
$= 400 + 60$
$= 460$

Break it down into pieces in which you can easily see the answer.

Do these in your head:

	Answers
23×70	$= 1{,}610$
3×18	$= 54$
9×42	$= 378$
8×56	$= 448$

Make up some more on your own and do them in your head. By practicing you'll be able to work more quickly.

b. ASSOCIATIVE LAW

In order to do addition quickly in your head, break down numbers into other simpler numbers that you can add quickly—like multiples of 10.

Example: $137 + 288$
$= (100 + 200) + (30 + 80) + (7 + 8)$
$= 300 + 110 + 15$
$= 425$

Example: 678 + 43
= (670 + 40) + (8 + 3)
= 710 + 11
= 721

2. Know the dividing rules.

a. any positive integer is divisible by 1 (we hope you already know this one).

b. even numbers are divisible by 2 (we hope you know this one, too).

c. numbers whose digits add up to multiples of 3 are divisible by 3.
Example: 186. Add the digits: 1 + 8 + 6 = 15 (a multiple of 3). So 186 is divisible by 3.

d. numbers whose last 2 digits form a number that is divisible by 4 are divisible by 4.
Example: 103,424 is divisible by 4 because 24 (last 2 digits) is.

e. numbers that end in 5 or 0 are divisible by 5.

f. numbers divisible by 2 *and* 3 are divisible by 6.

g. no rule for 7. Sorry, we don't make the rules!

h. numbers whose last 3 digits form a number that is divisible by 8 are divisible by 8.
Example: 10,496,832 is divisible by 8 because 832 (last 3 digits) is.

i. numbers whose digits add up to multiples of 9 are divisible by 9.
Example: 304,164. Add the digits:
3 + 4 + 1 + 6 + 4 = 18 (a multiple of 9). So 304,164 is divisible by 9.

j. numbers that end in 0 are divisible by 10.

Use the above shortcuts whenever you need to decide if something is a factor. Following are sample factor questions:

Which of the following are evenly divisible by 9?
(A) 183   (B) 4,761   (C) 108   (D) 2,503   (E) 17,621
(F) 113   (G) 1,098   (H) 72,000   (I) 144   (J) 153

Answers: (B), (C), (G), (H), (I), (J)

Which of the following is evenly divisible by 72?
(A) 9,324   (B) 6,075   (C) 99,144   (D) 130,761
(E) 120,613

Answer: (C). Divisible by 72 means divisible by 8 and by 9 (since $72 = 8 \times 9$). So both the 8 rule and the 9 rule must work. Notice that (B), (D), and (E) can be eliminated immediately since they're odd and therefore aren't divisible by 8. Answer (A) passes the 9 rule but fails the 8 rule.

3. Check the last digits.

If you're multiplying two numbers together, you can figure out what the last digit of the answer is without multiplying them completely: multiply the end numbers together and take the last digit of this product.

Example: $23 \times 257 =$ (A) 5,911
(B) 5,312
(C) 4,517
(D) 6,417
(E) 5,118

Without multiplying it out, let's do a last-digit check: 3×7 (the two last numbers) = 21; last digit = 1. Only choice (A) ends in 1; so the answer is (A).

4. Estimate!

Sometimes you don't need a precise number for an answer. You just need a basic idea of how big the answer will be. In these situations you can save time by rounding the numbers in the problem up or down so that you get numbers that are easier to work with. For example:

$49^2 =$ (A) 291
(B) 311
(C) 987

(D) 2401
(E) 23,210

49^2 can be rounded up to 50^2, which you can figure out in your head ($50^2 = 2,500$). The only answer that is close to 2,500 is (D), so it must be the right answer.

Estimation also helps if the last-digit check leaves you with a couple of choices. For example:

$31 \times 18 =$ (A) 318
(B) 9,508
(C) 558
(D) 551
(E) 583

The last digit check says it ends in 8, so eliminate (D) and (E). Estimate using $30 \times 20 = 600$. So the answer should be about 600: (A) is too small; (B) is way too big. The answer is (C), which is in the right range. So unless you're a bozo, you should be pretty happy.

The following are some rules of estimates:
a. If you round both numbers up, the estimate will be *larger* than the answer.
b. If you round both numbers down, the estimate will be *smaller* than the answer.
c. The farther you round, the greater the error in the estimate (i.e., 59 rounded to 60 will be closer than 55 rounded to 60).
d. If the answers are all in the same range, estimates will *not* do you any good (unless combined with a last digit check). However, if the answers are spread out, a last digit check could be unnecessary. But it's still a good idea if you have time.
e. Estimates don't work on problems involving pizza with anchovies. The difficulty involves calculus too arduous to demonstrate here, so just take our word for it—no

estimates on pizza with anchovies problems. Estimation still works on all other kinds of pizza problems.

5. Know squares and square roots.

Questions usually don't directly test squares and square roots, but sometimes you can see shortcuts by knowing them. Here's a table of the squares of numbers 11 to 20. Know them so that you can save time on your calculations.

Number	Square		Number	Square
11	121		17	289
12	144		18	324
13	169		19	361
14	196		20	400
15	225		(Also memorize	
16	256		$25^2 = 625$)	

Also notice that $(n + 1)^2 = n^2 + 2n + 1$. So the difference between two perfect squares is always an odd number ($2n + 1$). Because of this, you can always figure out the next perfect square just by adding the ($2n + 1$).

Example: We know $10^2 = 100$,
so $11^2 = 100 + 20 + 1 = 121$

Sample Questions

Here are some problems that are intended to make you feel happy about yourself. If they don't, don't worry: math isn't everything. Use the tricks outlined above to help cut down your test-taking time. If you get them wrong, work more slowly and carefully.

1. 249 × 249 = (A) 62,509   (B) 62,001   (C) 63,001
   (D) 62,501

2. 13 × 17 = (A) 253   (B) 242   (C) 230   (D) 228
   (E) 221

3. What is $1,001^2$?
   (A) 10,201
   (B) 1,002,001
   (C) 100,100
   (D) 101,101
   (E) 10,011,001

4. A square has an area of 144. How long is the side of the next larger square with integral side?
   (A) 11
   (B) 12
   (C) 13
   (D) 14
   (E) None of the above

Answers:
1. (B). Estimate: $250 \times 250 = 62,500$; last digit = 1. Note: We rounded both numbers up, so our estimate (62,500) must be *larger* than the actual answer.
2. (E). Last digit = 1.
3. (B). Estimate: $(1,000)^2 = 1,000,000$. (B) is the only answer in this range.
4. (C). $\sqrt{144} = 12$; 13 is the next larger integer. Notice that you didn't need to find the area—only the length of the side. This is one of those problems where knowing squares and square roots helps.

FRACTIONS/ UNITS

You've done a lot of fractions in math class, so you know, more or less, how to work with them. But do you know what a fraction *means*? Do you completely understand that $\frac{3}{5}$ not only means *three–fifths*, but also means 3 *divided by* 5? Also, do you completely understand that miles/hour means *miles divided by hours*? If not, read this section carefully and then read it again. Fractions and units are the most important things to master for the math SAT.

The Meaning of a Fraction

The following problem will illustrate why *three–fifths* and *3 divided by 5* are the same thing.

The Quiche Problem

Rambo, Magnum, Mr. T, Hulk Hogan, and Don Johnson are having dinner together. They order 3 quiches, which they plan to divide equally. How much quiche does each person get?

Here's a three-step solution to this problem:

Step 1: Cut the first quiche into 5 equal pieces (i.e., into fifths) and give 1 piece to each person.

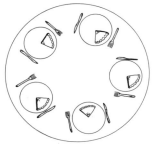

Step 2: Do the same thing to the second quiche:

Step 3: Do the same thing to the third quiche:

Now, as you can see, everyone has 3 slices of quiche. Each slice is a fifth of a quiche, so everyone has three–fifths (⅗) of a quiche. So, 3 quiches were divided equally among 5 people to give each person ⅗ of a quiche.

This is what this problem was designed to demonstrate—that 3 divided by 5 and ⅗ are the same thing: 3 quiches divided by 5 people = ⅗ of a quiche per person. Read this paragraph over and over again until you understand it. Then go eat some quiche.

Complex Fractions

The Serpent loves testing your ability to work with fractions by creating problems that contain complex fractions. A complex fraction is a regular fraction divided by another regular fraction. Here are some examples of complex fractions:

$$\frac{3/5}{7/13} \quad \text{or} \quad \frac{a/b}{c/d} \quad \text{or} \quad \frac{\text{hours/mile}}{\text{wombat/person}}$$

Since complex fractions are a pain in the neck, you want to make them into regular fractions. There is a simple rule for simplifying complex fractions.

Simple Rule: Put the bottom of the lower with the top of the upper and the top of the lower with the bottom of the upper.

Simple? Well, actually it is. You just have to know where all of the uppers and lowers and bottoms and tops are. Label the complex fraction like this:

$$\text{upper} \left\{ \frac{\text{top of the upper}}{\text{bottom of the upper}} \right.$$
$$\text{lower} \left\{ \frac{\text{top of the lower}}{\text{bottom of the lower}} \right.$$

What the Simple Rule says is that you can simplify any complex fraction by moving the bottom of the lower up to the top of the upper and the top of the lower to the bottom of the upper. Here's what the simple rule looks like:

$$\frac{(\text{top of upper}) \times (\text{bottom of lower})}{(\text{bottom of upper}) \times (\text{top of lower})}$$

Here are some problems. Make each complex fraction into a simple (regular) fraction. Practice the simple rule.

1. $\dfrac{3/5}{4/7} = ?$

    You should immediately rewrite this as

    $$\frac{3 \times 7}{5 \times 4}$$

2. $\dfrac{a/b}{c/d} = ?$

    You should immediately rewrite this as:

    $$\frac{a \times d}{b \times c}$$

3. $\dfrac{\text{quiches/person}}{\text{brains/tofu}}$

    You should immediately rewrite this as:

    $$\frac{\text{quiches} \times \text{tofu}}{\text{person} \times \text{brains}}$$

Word Fractions (Units)

Miles per hour is a way that we measure speed. You've probably seen miles per hour written as a fraction: miles/hour. Using the quiche problem, we just confirmed that *fractions* mean "division." So *miles per hour* must mean "miles divided by hours." But what does that mean? How do you divide a mile by an hour? What does it mean to travel 400 miles divided by hours? The following problem will attempt to answer all of these questions.

The Tofu Problem

After our quiche-eaters have finished eating, they get in the car to go to a frozen-tofu dessert shop. The tofu shop is 500 miles away. If it takes them 10 hours to get there, what was their average speed?

Answer: The key is to realize that if they drive 500 miles in 10 hours then they have 500 miles to divide among 10 hours of driving. (It's just like having 3 quiches to divide among 5 people.) So rewrite it as:

$$\frac{500 \text{ miles}}{10 \text{ hours}} = \frac{50 \text{ miles}}{1 \text{ hour}} = 50 \text{ miles/hour}$$

Now you know why *miles per hour* is the same thing as miles/hour.

Units

Anything that you can count or measure will have a unit associated with it. *Pounds* are units, *miles* are units, *hours* are units, *miles/hour* are units, even *noodles* can be units if you are counting or measuring with noodles.

Knowing the tricks of working with units can help you do problems faster and can show you how to do problems that you otherwise wouldn't know how to do. The rule for working with units is that you can multiply and divide them just as you would numbers. For example, when you multiply (or divide) fractions containing units you can cancel units in the numerator with units in the denominator:

$$\frac{10 \text{ miles}}{1 \text{ hour}} \times 5 \text{ hours} = 50 \text{ miles}$$

$$\frac{10 \text{ pizzas}}{3 \text{ people}} \times 7 \text{ people} = 70/3 \text{ pizzas}$$

And you can divide using the simple rule:

$$\frac{\dfrac{5 \text{ pounds}}{\text{chicken}}}{\dfrac{3 \text{ chickens}}{10 \text{ McNuggets}}} = \frac{50 \text{ pounds} \times \text{McNuggets}}{3 \text{ (chickens)}^2}$$

After some practice, multiplying and dividing units will be as simple and as natural to you as multiplying and dividing numbers.

We will now do a few practice problems from real SATs that show the procedure for doing units problems. (The following problems are from pages 23 and 62 of *6 SATs*.)

2. A gasoline tank on a certain tractor holds 16 gallons. If the tractor requires 7 gallons to plow 3 acres, how many acres can the tractor plow with a tankful of gasoline?

   (A) 6⁶/₇ (B) 7⅙ (C) 7⅓ (D) 10⅔ (E) 37⅓

There are two steps to all units problems:
1. Figure out what information they give you in the problem.
2. Pick, from only three options, what to do with that information.

Step 1: Figure out the information given.

1. "7 gallons to plow 3 acres" $= \dfrac{7 \text{ gallons}}{3 \text{ acres}}$

2. "A gasoline tank holds 16 gallons" = 16 gallons

3. "How many acres?" means. . . answer in *acres*.

Step 2: Do the right thing with the information given.

In all units problems, you have three options for what to do with the given information. You can:

1. Multiply the first thing × the second thing.
2. Divide the first thing/the second thing.
3. Divide the second thing/the first thing.

The great thing about units problems is that it is not necessary to understand what's going on in order to know which of the three options to use. You try them all and only one is going to work out correctly. This is because the answer *must* be in acres and only one of the three options is going to give an answer in acres. So, we try the three options:

1. $\dfrac{7 \text{ gallons}}{3 \text{ acres}} \times 16 \text{ gallons} = \dfrac{(16 \times 7) \text{ gallons}^2}{3 \text{ acres}}$

Nope! The answer has to be in terms of acres, not in terms of $\dfrac{\text{gallons}^2}{\text{acres}}$.

2. $\dfrac{\dfrac{7 \text{ gallons}}{3 \text{ acres}}}{16 \text{ gallons}} = \dfrac{7 \text{ gallons}}{3 \text{ acres} \times 16 \text{ gallons}}$

Nope! We want acres in the numerator.

3. $\dfrac{16 \text{ gallons}}{\dfrac{7 \text{ gallons}}{3 \text{ acres}}} = \dfrac{16 \text{ gallons} \times 3 \text{ acres}}{7 \text{ gallons}} = 6\tfrac{6}{7} \text{ acres}$

Yes! This is the right answer. Notice that we didn't even have to figure out what the problem was all about; we just tried the three options and the units worked out correctly on the third try.

Let's do another one:

11. A mechanic can install carburetors in 3 cars every 4

hours. At that rate, how long will it take the mechanic to install carburetors in 5 cars?

(A) 6 hrs. 20 min.
(B) 6 hrs. 40 min.
(C) 7 hrs. 15 min.
(D) 7 hrs. 30 min.
(E) 7 hrs. 45 min.

Step 1: Figure out the information given.

$$\text{``3 cars every 4 hours''} = \frac{3 \text{ cars}}{4 \text{ hours}}$$

$$\text{``install in 5 cars''} \quad = \quad 5 \text{ cars}$$

Because the answer choices are in terms of hours and minutes, and because the question asks, "How long will it take?" the answer will be in terms of hours and minutes.

Step 2: Do the right thing with the information given.
Try the three options. This time we won't even worry about the numbers. All we care about is that the answer be in terms of the unit "hours."

1. $\dfrac{3 \text{ cars}}{4 \text{ hours}} \times 5 \text{ cars}$

Nope. Gives answer in cars^2/hour.

2. $\dfrac{\dfrac{3 \text{ cars}}{4 \text{ hours}}}{5 \text{ cars}}$

Nope. Gives answer in 1/hours. We want the hours in the numerator.

So, sure enough, the third option works:

$$3. \quad \frac{\dfrac{5 \text{ cars}}{3 \text{ cars}}}{4 \text{ hours}} = \frac{5 \text{ cars} \times 4 \text{ hours}}{3 \text{ cars}} = 20/3 \text{ hours}$$

$$= 6 \text{ hrs. } 40 \text{ min.}$$

Sometimes units problems require more than one operation. For example, if you want to calculate how many seconds there are in a day, you would do the following set of operations:

$$\frac{60 \text{ sec}}{\text{min}} \times \frac{60 \text{ min}}{\text{hour}} \times \frac{24 \text{ hours}}{\text{day}} = \frac{60 \times 60 \times 24 \text{ sec}}{\text{day}}$$

Note that even if you hadn't known that the right way to do this problem was to multiply these quantities together, you could have figured it out by trying all the possibilities of dividing and multiplying. Only one of those possibilities would have given an answer in terms of seconds/day.

And now we break for a commercial...

Don't you hate it when rabid elephants attack you and steal your pencils? I do. On the crucial day of my test, I was carrying no fewer than eight number 2 pencils and this tremendous elephant, foaming at the mouth, lunged out of the test center and grabbed my writing implements. I was ticked off.

But then I decided to try new improved Oxford Anti-Elephant soap. It not only cleans and softens my skin but also keeps those pesky pachyderms away. Now I can carry as many pencils with me as I like, and it's improved my whole life.

Well, some of my life. Actually, the point of this message is to remind you to have enough number 2 pencils around when you take your test. Also, we wanted to give you a break from reading about math—after all, math is not the most exciting material available for perusal.

Now, get back to work!

WORD PROBLEMS

You really don't need to know much more than the basics to get through the word problems—but you do need to know how to think. It turns out that a lot of the math questions deal more with words than with actual math. Often the hard part is translating the words into math. You see,

$$378,614 \times 2 + 4/136,319 = y$$

looks like a hell of a problem. But it isn't that bad because it's just numbers and you can do it knowing only how to add, multiply, and divide. You don't really have to think—you just have to apply the skills you've (supposedly) known since second grade.

The really hateful questions are the word problems:

> Bill has four apples and is 18 years old. Sue has 25% more apples than Bill and is 1/3 as old. Alex had twice as many apples as Sue (and is 3/2 as old), but he gave one of his apples to Bill (and that's why Bill has four instead of three).
>
> For which individual is the ratio of apples/age the greatest?

Not only do you need to know about ratios and percentage and addition and stuff, but you also need to know how to translate the words into math. (The answer is Alex, by the way.)

So let's start with words—Okay? (Put the Raisinettes away and pay attention.)

Words

The following are a bunch of rules for how to change confusing words into easy to understand numbers and mathematical symbols.

Rule #1. *Of* **usually means multiply.** Like "½ *of y*" means multiplying ½ times *y*.

Rule #2. *Exceeds by* **or** *is greater than by* **means subtract.**

Examples: *x* exceeds *y* by 7 means $x - y = 7$

x is greater than *y* by 7 means $x - y = 7$

Rule #3. *Percent* **(%) usually goes with** *of.* Remember that *per cent* means *per hundred*, so a percent problem is really just a problem with fractions. They tell you the numerator and give you the "%" sign, which you translate into meaning "over one hundred." For example, 25% is really $^{25}/_{100}$, which is a fraction.

25% of *y* becomes

$^{25}/_{100}$ of *y* (remember *of* means multiply), so it's

$^{25}/_{100} \times y$

Do the same thing for percentages greater than 100%. For instance, 250% means $^{250}/_{100}$.

Rule #4. But wait, there's *more.* **Percent can be made trickier with the word** *more.* If Sue has 25% *more* apples than Bill, then she has *as many* apples as Bill *plus* 25% more.

So the word *more* can be broken down into: *As many* —— *plus* ——.

But we can do better than apples:

a. Bill has exactly 8 pairs of sexy underwear.

b. Sue has 50% more pairs of underwear than Bill.

c. 75% of Sue's total collection of underwear is sexy.

Who has more sexy underwear? (Don't get distracted.)

Here's the answer: By Rule #4, Sue has *as many* pairs as Bill *plus* 50%.

So, Sue has 8 pairs + $^{50}/_{100}$ of 8.

Sue has $8 + 4 = 12$ pairs of underwear.

75% of her 12 total pairs of underwear is sexy.

Using Rule #3, this becomes $^{75}/_{100}$ of 12.

And finally using Rule #1, this becomes $^{75}/_{100} \times 12 = 9$.

Sue has 9 pairs of sexy underwear and Bill has 8, so Sue has more. But they both have about as much fun.

Rule #5. *Ratio*—**Okay, so what's a ratio? A ratio is a comparison (yep—just like in the analogy questions).** If you say $y > x$ then you're comparing y and x and finding out that y is larger than x. (And you might ask, who really cares?) But $y > x$ is not a ratio. Ratios involve "division comparisons":

"the ratio of y to x is 5" means $y/x = 5$

Here, y is being compared to x. Again y is bigger—but now we know that y is 5 times bigger. (Wow. Excitement.) This expression could also be written as:

"y is to x as 5 is to 1" or $y:x$ as $5:1$

Okay, well, how *is* 5 to 1? 5 *is* five times as big as one (obviously). So y is five times x, get it?

Rule #6. *Average*—**an average is a number that is an approximation for all the numbers in a group.**

Average $= (a + b + c + d\ldots)/n$ where a, b, c, d,... are the numbers, and n is the number of numbers being averaged. For example, the average of 3, 5, 6, 7 is:

$A = (3 + 5 + 6 + 7)/4 = 5\frac{1}{4}$.

Notice that $n = 4$ since there are four numbers in the group. Sometimes figuring out what n is can be tricky: Here's an example of such a problem:

Larry's average for the first three tests was 90%; his average for the next two was 80%. What was his overall average?

To find n in this problem you have to notice that there are *five* test scores to average: the first three can be thought of as 90s, the next two as 80s, and the average becomes:

$A = (90 + 90 + 90 + 80 + 80)/5 = 86\%$

If you tried to do this by averaging 80% and 90% you'd

be wrong. And Larry would have been upset because you gave him an 85% instead of an 86%.

1. The ratio of feet to shoes in this room is 3 to 1. The number of beings is 8 humans and 2 rats (unshod). How many shoes are there total?

All right. Let's set it up like a *math* problem:

a. By Rule #5 (ratio): feet/shoes = 3/1

b. number of feet = 8 humans (at 2 feet each) =   16
                    2 rats (at 4 feet each) =   +   8
                                number of feet =   24

c. Replace the word *feet* in the first step with the number 24 to get:
    24/shoes = 3/1. Now, solve for shoes. Shoes = 8.
    Why? Because 24/8 = 3/1 right? Or 24 : 8 = 3 : 1 (same thing—Rule #5).

All right, that was a stupid problem. They're usually not that weird on the actual test.

2. 5 is what percent of 10?

"Wait—I haven't done this!" you moan. Just relax—you can do it with what you already know. Change the question around to read:

What percent of 10 is 5?

Of means multiply—so something *times* 10 is 5. You should be able to figure out that the something is ½. (Right? ½ × 10 is 5, isn't it?) And ½ is 50%, so that's the answer: 5 is 50% of 10.

Another way to set this up is using a ratio:

5 is to 10 as x is to 100
$5 : 10 :: x : 100$
$5/10 = x/100$

And solve for x.

3. On a map, if one inch represents thirty miles, then how many inches represent 75 miles?

This is a thinly disguised ratio problem—the key word here is *represent*. The problem can be translated to look like this:

$$1 \text{ inch} : 30 \text{ miles} :: x \text{ inches} : 75 \text{ miles}$$
$$1/30 = x/75$$

Solving for x gives us $x = 2 \, 1/2$ inches.

4. Mary's average salary for her first 6 years of work was $15,000; her average salary for the next 2 years was $16,000. What was her average salary over the entire 8 years?

Notice that n for this problem is 8; the average is:

$$A = (6 \times 15,000 + 2 \times 16,000)/8 = \$15,250$$

5. If Paul ate 300% more pizza than Manek ate, and Manek ate an entire pizza, then how many pizzas did Paul eat?

Paul ate *as many* pizzas as Manek *plus* 300%.
So Paul ate ONE pizza PLUS 300% of one.
So Paul ate FOUR PIZZAS! (Paul, you glutton.)

Advanced Math For Word Problems

The Moving People Problem
　　These questions are famous. They have no relevance to anything, really, but involve people making work for themselves by going places and coming back again for no apparent reason.

A man in a bus travels 4 miles in 3 minutes. Then he gets out of the bus and walks back to his starting point, taking $9/20$ hour. What was his average speed for the whole trip?
Answer: 16 miles/hour

The best way to deal with this type of word problem is to draw a picture, with distances and times (like this):

$$= \frac{\text{4 miles in 3 min by bus } + \text{ 4 miles in 27 min walking}}{\text{8 miles in 30 minutes total}}$$

Get it? Add up total miles, divide by total time, and you'll like totally get the answer.

Example:
A boat travels 3 miles north, 4 miles east, and then sinks. If it sank to a depth of 1 mile, then how far is it from its starting point?
Use the Pythagorean theorem and a picture to get the answer.

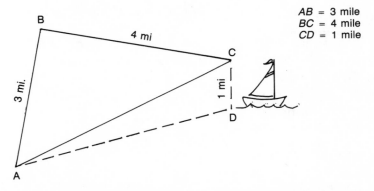

AB = 3 mile
BC = 4 mile
CD = 1 mile

Point A is where the boat began. It sailed 3 miles north to point B then 4 miles east to point C. It then sank 1 mile to point D. The distance of the boat from its starting point is AD. So you must solve for AD, but first you must figure the distance of the hypotenuse, AC, of the triangle ABC.

$$AC^2 = AB^2 + BC^2$$
$$AC^2 = 3^2\text{mi} + 4^2\text{mi}$$
$$AC^2 = 25 \text{ mi}$$
$$\sqrt{AC^2} = \sqrt{25} \text{ mi}$$
$$AC = 5 \text{ mi}$$

Now you're ready to solve for AD, the hypotenuse of triangle ACD:

$$AD^2 = AC^2 + CD^2$$
$$AD^2 = 5^2\text{mi} + 1^2\text{mi}$$
$$AD^2 = 26 \text{ mi}$$
$$\sqrt{AD^2} = \sqrt{26} \text{ mi}$$
$$AD = \sqrt{26} \text{ mi}$$

So, the distance of the boat from its starting point is 5.1 miles.

A man's goldfish swims around the edge of its cylindrical fishtank, which has a radius of 1 meter (it's a big fishtank), at a rate of 1 lap per 30 seconds. How long does it take the fish to swim 32π meters, if after every 4 laps the fish takes a 5-second break to eat some Chiclets? (Include the final break.)

(A) 16 minutes
(B) 500 minutes
(C) 8⅓ minutes
(D) 32 minutes
(E) $30/32\pi$ minutes

Answer: (C)

Example:
A man can do a job in h hours and is paid $8 an hour. He works for $h/4$ hours and then is forced into early retirement due to having a large gold brick dropped on him from a height of 20 feet. His employer hires 2 people to finish the job—one of whom could do the whole job in $2h$ hours working alone, the other in $3h$ hours (each is paid $4 an hour). How much must the employer pay for the entire job if he gives the injured man a pension of $2.58?

(A) $8 + 16$h$ + $2.58
(B) 9.2h dollars + $2.58

(C) .36*h* dollars + $2.58

(D) 32*h* dollars + $2.58

(E) (*h*/4) × 8 dollars + ¾ × *h* × 4 dollars

Answer: (B)

Note: This question is too hard to be asked, so don't freak—but do attempt to solve it yourself. The math itself isn't rough, it's just figuring out how to set it up that's difficult.

Since man #1 worked $h/4$ hours, he did ¼ of the job; the remaining ¾ must be done by his two replacements. Since worker #2 takes 2*h* hours to do it all, he could do $\frac{1}{2h}$ of the job per hour. Similarly, worker #3 completes $\frac{1}{3h}$ of the job per hour. Together they can do $\frac{1}{2h} + \frac{1}{3h}$ in an hour. But how many hours does it take them to complete the remaining ¾ of the job?

$$(1/2h + 1/3h)x = 3/4$$
$$(1/2 + 1/3)x = (3/4)h$$
$$\frac{3 + 2}{6}x = (3/4)h$$
$$x = (18/20)h$$
$$x = (9h/10) \text{ hours}$$

Now you can compute the payroll:

worker #1:

h/4 hours @ $8/hour = *h*/4 × $8	=	2*h* dollars

worker #2:

9*h*/10 hours @ $4/hour = 9*h*/10 × $4	=	3.6*h* dollars

worker #3: . . . same as worker #2 . . . = 3.6*h* dollars

. . . and don't forget the pension . . . = $2.58

for a grand total of: 9.2*h* dollars + $2.58

End Advanced Math

Enough of this math stuff—the SAT requires fast thinking in difficult situations. So here's a scenario—you have three seconds to come up with the appropriate response.

A psychotic iguana with a bottle of dishwashing detergent is chasing you and gaining every second. The soft grass you're running on barefoot suddenly ends and you're faced with the option of treading on a minefield strewn with broken glass or walking across a river of flowing lava. Which do you choose?

Answer: Neither. What are you, stupid? I'd much rather face an iguana (even a psychotic one with detergent) than deal with a minefield or hot lava. So remember, if you really *don't* like any of your choices, then, "it cannot be determined from the information given," is an option.

EQUATIONS

The rule for equations is *do it to both sides*. We don't care what *it* is, but do it to both sides. That keeps everything nice and equal. So if your lover is your enemy:

(lover = enemy)

and you want to kill your enemy, you have to kill your lover as well:

(kill your lover = kill your enemy)

There. Nice and equal. Well, equal, anyway.

So if you have

$$x + 36 = 40$$

and you want to solve for *x*, then do it like this. Subtract 36 from the left *and* subtract 36 from the right to get

$$x + 36 - 36 = 40 - 36 \text{ which means that } x = 4.$$

Now check it by substituting 4 for *x* in the original expression:

$$4 + 36 = 40$$
$$40 = 40 \quad \text{Bingo!}$$

Here are some examples:

1. $12x = 24$ Divide both sides by 12 to get $x = 2$

2. $3x + 4 = 28$
   Subtract 4 from both sides to get $3x = 24$
   Divide both sides by 3 to get $x = 8$

3. Solve for fish:

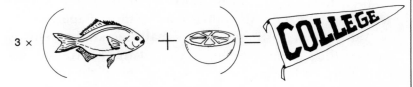

   $3x$ (fish + grapefruit) = college
   Divide both sides by 3:
   fish + grapefruit = college/3
   subtract grapefruit from both sides:
   fish = college/3 − grapefruit

   Okay. "Number 3 was a moronic question," you might say to yourself. Yes. It was. But they ask similar questions on the SAT just to see if you know these rules. They use x, y, and z more than they use fish and grapefruit, but it's the same basic idea.

4. x less $y = 17$
   What is $y + 12$?

   (A) x
   (B) $x + 5$
   (C) $x - 5$
   (D) It cannot be determined from the information
       given.
   Answer: (C)

5. x plus 3 minus y = 10
   Solve for x in terms of y

   (A) y + 7
   (B) y + 3
   (C) y − 7
   (D) 10 − y
   (E) It cannot be determined from the information given.
   Answer: (A)

Paper, people often say, is a good thing. (This is our chance to wax philosophical.) Without paper, where would we all be? On the other hand, without paper, where would the Evil Testing Serpent's math section be? This is one of life's great problems—one of the contradictions built into the fabric of the universe—one of the questions that has been puzzled over by many great minds since the discovery of Retsyn.

Fortunately, you don't have to answer that question—you just have to do math. So go now into the world and do a few math sections from *10 SATs*. It will uplift your spirit.

First off, familiarize yourself with the following defini-tions, laws, and formulas:

Congruent angles: Have equal numbers of degrees. (They fit perfectly over each other.)

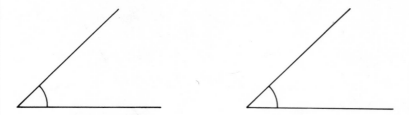

Complementary angles: Add up to 90 degrees of arc. (If they look complementary, and it doesn't say "not drawn to scale," they probably are complementary. Don't bother proving it to yourself if you're pressed for time.)

Supplementary angles: Add up to 180 degrees of arc. (If they look supplementary, they probably are.)

Parallel lines cut by another line: These things are full of

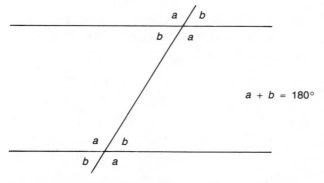

congruent and supplementary angles. You could try to memorize which pairs of angles are congruent and which pairs are supplementary, but why bother? The ones that look supplementary are supplementary, and the ones that look congruent are congruent.

Parallelogram: Opposite sides are parallel. Parallelo-grams have two pairs of *equal* (or *congruent*) angles and four pairs of *supplementary* angles. In the diagram, the

GEOMETRY PROBLEMS

Basic Math For Geometry

General Note:
Here's a tip that may help you not only with geometry problems but with other parts of the math test as well. If the caption for a di-agram says "not drawn to scale," then the first thing you should do is make a quick sketch that *is* to scale. One of the reasons they don't draw things to scale is to obscure the answer. So draw it to scale—nothing elaborate, nothing time-consuming. Just a quick sketch.

ones that look equal are equal and the ones that look supplementary are supplementary.

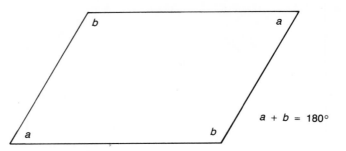

$a + b = 180°$

Similar triangles: Well, boys and girls, now it's time to give you some exciting insights into similar triangles. After extensive research, we've decided that there is nothing exciting about similar triangles. In fact, there's been nothing *new* in similar triangles for something over 2,000 years—but (and this is the incredible part) they're still in fashion with the ETS. So don your toga and get psyched for a bacchanalian triangle party!

What are similar triangles? Similar triangles are the same triangle in different sizes. Here, for example, are two similar triangles:

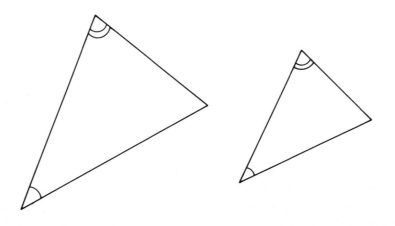

Continuing along this line of thought, here are two similar fish:

Same shape, different sizes (size 6 and size 10).

The technical way to think about similar triangles is that all three angles that make up each triangle have the same measure. And if you think about it, knowing that *two* of the three angles are the same is enough to ensure that *all three* are the same, since the angles of a triangle add up to 180°.

So, to jump right in here, what is the measure of angle *x* if A and B are similar triangles?

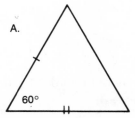

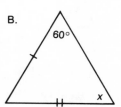

Answer: $x = 60°$. Why? Because all three angles are 60° (since $60 + 60 + 60 = 180°$).

Here's another one:
If AB ∥ CD, then what is ⊖?

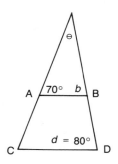

Answer: ⊖ = 30°. The key here is the parallel lines. Remember the congruent angles involved with parallel lines? Sure you do. So think of them when looking at the picture: angle *b* must be the same as angle *d*, namely 80°. Which brings us to a *Similar Triangle Rule:*

The top triangle is similar to the big triangle if their bases are parallel (see picture).

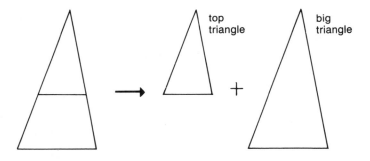

Got it? So if you see a triangle intersected by a line parallel to its base, the two triangles are similar.

Circles:

area $= (\pi \times r^2)$

circumference $= (2 \times \pi \times r)$

arc $=$ measure of central angle

Well, what the hell is that? Let us show you:

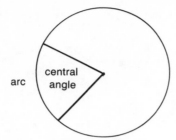

arc $= 2 \times$ measure of inscribed angle

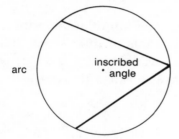

inscribed angle—*on* the circle

Area in general is a length times a width.

Rectangle: area $= b \times h$ (*b* is base and *h* is height, or vice versa)

Triangle: area $= \frac{1}{2} \times b \times h$. The $\frac{1}{2}$ comes in because a triangle is $\frac{1}{2}$ as large as a rectangle with the same base and height.

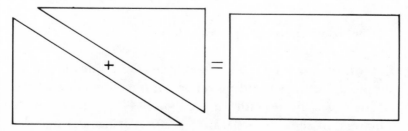

Circle: area = $\pi \times r^2$

Volume in general is an area times a height.

Rectangular solid: volume = length × width × height

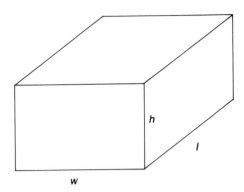

   Surface area, or the amount of area on the surface of the solid, is often seen as lots of little areas added up.

   Rectangular solid: surface area = $2 \times l \times w + 2 \times h \times w + 2 \times h \times l$. Why? Because there are three different pairs of sides.

   Cylinder: surface area = $2 \times \pi \times r^2 + 2 \times \pi \times r \times h$. The $2 \times \pi \times r^2$ are the two ends (circles), and the $2 \times \pi \times r \times h$ is the rectangle you get if you unroll the side.

   Smell: Usually smell isn't tested on the SAT, but I think it's sort of cool that it's supposed to be related to shape. And remember the word *fetid,* which means *smelly.*

   Note: Some of these formulas are actually printed in the SAT exam instructions. So, if you draw a blank, scan the instructions for the formula you need.

   Now, solve these sample problems:

1. Jennifer wants to build a fence (God knows why—people are always building fences in questions like these) to enclose a circle with an area of $144 \times \pi$. How much fencing will she need? (Draw a picture. It usually helps.)

Amount of fence = circumference
Circumference = $2 \times \pi \times r$

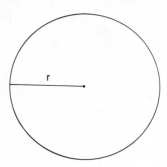

Well, we can't solve it without knowing the radius. So, find the radius from the known area ($144 \times \pi$).

$$144 \times \pi = \pi \times r^2$$
$$r^2 = 144$$
$$r = 12$$

So she needs $2 \times \pi \times r = 2 \times \pi \times 12 = 24 \times \pi$ fence. She also needs a psychoanalyst.

2. Which angles are equal in this picture?

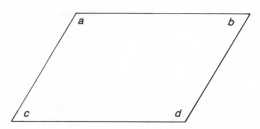

Answer: (a, d) and (c, b) because in a parallelogram, opposite angles are equal.

Which are supplementary?
Answer: (a, c); (b, d); (a, b); and (c, d) because consecutive angles are supplementary.

But don't prove it each time. Just know it by looking.

3. What is the measure of angle *x*?

Notice that angle *y* and 150° form a straight line, so they are supplementary. Since $y + 150° = 180°$, $y = 30°$. Now use the sum of the angles of the triangle to solve for *x*.

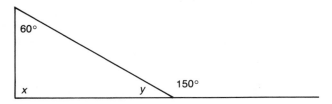

Answer: 90°

4. What is the measure of angle *x*?

The 40° angle is *inscribed*, so the arc shown is 80°, as is, therefore, central angle *x*.

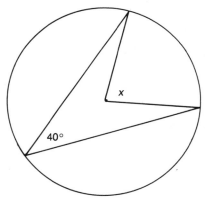

Answer: 80°

5. What is the measure of angle *x*?

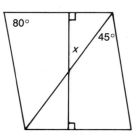

Just break down the figure into the following components to find x.

First:

These angles are supplementary, therefore: $y = 100°$

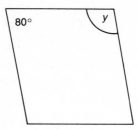

Second:

$z + 45° = y = 100°$
$z = 55°$

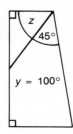

Finally:

$x + 55° + 90° = 180°$
$x = 35°$

Answer: 35°

The above three questions were worded the same, yet they dealt with different geometric shapes. It's important that you learn to deal with angle measures in a variety of geometric figures.

Advanced Math for Geometry

The advanced geometry involves a little more thinking and a whole bunch of tricks.

The Weird Geometry Questions

Some of the nastier questions involve weird geometry—geometry that is hard to figure out at first from the diagrams—but which turns out to be really easy if you look hard enough. The main strategy is to separate the big shape into lots of little shapes, and then solve them one by one.

1.

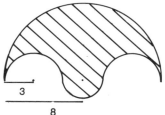

What is the area of the shaded thing?
Well, what the hell is it? There's no formula for things like that, but realize that it's really not so bad.

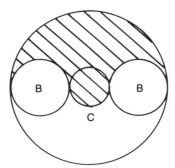

A: radius = 8
B: *r* = 3
C: *r* = 2

This shape is just a bunch of circles—the big one (A), two medium ones (B) and the small one (C). You know the formula for the area of a circle ($\pi \times r^2$), so you can solve this thing. (The answer is $\frac{1}{2}(64\pi - 18\pi + 4\pi) = 25\pi$. Pretty cool, no?)

2.

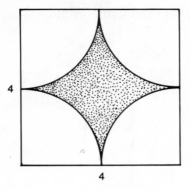

Again, find the shaded area (left over when you cut quarter circles out of a square). Solve for the area of the square minus $4 \times \triangle$. Four quarter circles equals one whole circle, therefore the area of the shaded area equals the area of the square minus the area of a circle with a radius of 2.

Answer: $16 - 4\pi$

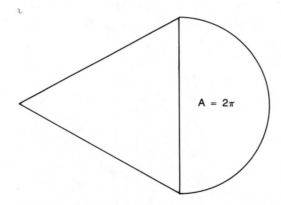

The area of the semicircle is 2π. What is the area of the equilateral triangle? Remember: The area of an equilateral triangle of side s is

$$A = \frac{s^2\sqrt{3}}{4}$$

(If you don't remember or never learned this, learn it now.)

Answer: $4\sqrt{3}$

4. What is the volume of this thing?

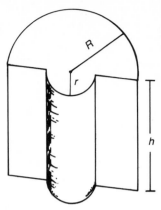

Answer: $\pi \times h/2(R^2 + r^2)$
What is its total surface area?
Answer: $\pi(R^2 + r^2) + 2h(R - r) + \pi Rh + \pi rh$

Note: This question is probably too long and involved for the SAT. But you never know. Make sure at least that you know where the answer comes from: they could ask for part of it.

5. What's the shaded area?

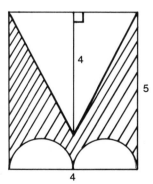

Answer: $20 - \pi - 8 = 12 - \pi$

Coordinate Geometry Questions
We hate these. There's not much you can do except know your stuff. Fortunately, there isn't too much asked.

Remember:

Pythagorean theorem: $a^2 + b^2 = c^2$

distance between a point (a, b) and a point (x, y) in a plane is $d = \sqrt{(y - b)^2 + (x - a)^2}$

slope of line m, where $y = mx + b$ (b is y – intercept)

1. A circle of radius 3 is centered at the origin.

a. What is the closest distance from the circle to the line with equation $y = 6$?

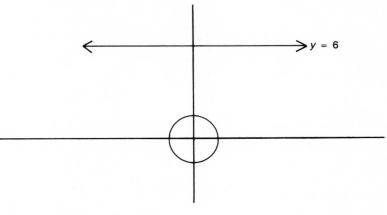

(A) zero

(B) 3

(C) (3 − 6)

(D) 6

(E) 9

Draw a picture—make sure you can do graphs. Remember: The equation for a circle is

$$(x - a)^2 + (y - b)^2 = r^2$$

where (a, b) is the center, r is the radius.

Answer: (B)

b. What is the area of the intersection of the circle $x^2 + y^2 = 8$ and the rectangle with vertices at (0, 0), (− 2, 2) and (4, 4)?

(A) 16
(B) (3.14) × 8
(C) 2 π
(D) π/4
(E) 16 − 8 π

Make a quick sketch. It's easy—just locate the rectangle and circle and notice that their intersection is a quarter of the circle.

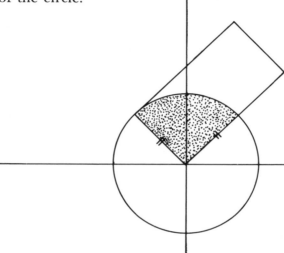

End Advanced Math

Answer: (C)

QUANTITATIVE COMPARISONS

Okay, the idea behind quantitative comparison questions is that you've never seen them before—the Serpent made up something so ridiculous that no one else would ever use it.

The way quantitative comparison works is as follows:

For each problem you are given two expressions: *stuff A* and *stuff B*. The object is to pick which is bigger (A or B). Pick (C) if they are equal and (D) if you can't tell (meaning *Einstein couldn't tell*).

Note: Don't be a dope and choose (E). Even if (E) is on your answer sheet, it is not a choice.

The trick is that you *DON'T* always need to *solve* A or B; all you have to know is which one is bigger. For example:

$$A \qquad\qquad\qquad\qquad\qquad\qquad B$$
$$23{,}160 \times (400{,}306{,}124 + 936{,}124{,}131) \qquad 456/3$$

It doesn't take much to figure out that A is bigger, and *NO WAY* should you add and multiply it out. That would be masochistic. Try this:

$$A \qquad\qquad\qquad\qquad B$$
$$1/2 + 1/17 + 1/7 \qquad 1/20 + 1/5 + 1/8$$

Again, A is bigger. Without solving, notice that:

$$1/2 > 1/5$$
$$1/17 > 1/20$$
$$1/7 > 1/8$$

So every fraction on the left is bigger than a corresponding fraction on the right and therefore the sum on the left side is bigger.

Note: Never select choice (D) if there is no unknown variable in the question, because if there is no unknown in the problem, then there must be enough information to decide which is bigger.

PLUGGING IN

As we pointed out earlier, you don't have to find answers for everything in the quantitative comparison section, all you have to do is figure out if A or B is bigger. If the things that you're comparing are algebraic statements, then sometimes the fastest way to do this is to plug in numbers and see which statement comes out bigger. The Evil Testing Serpent wants you to do this. But he wants you to do it wrong. For example:

$$A \qquad\qquad\qquad B$$
$$x^2 \qquad\qquad\qquad x^3$$

The ETS wants you to choose (B), because he thinks you'll say to yourself, "Hmmm...which is bigger, 10^2 or 10^3? I guess 10^3 is bigger, so the answer is (B)." The correct answer is (D). Why? Because although B is bigger when x is greater than 1, A is greater when x is less than 1:

$$(1/2)^2 = 1/4 \qquad\qquad (1/2)^3 = 1/8$$

The moral of the story is: If you're using the plug-in method, always plug in numbers greater than 1, numbers between 1 and 0, 1 itself, 0, and a negative number. Always means *ALWAYS*. Make sure that you do this every time you plug in!

THE FUNNY SYMBOL QUESTION

As if the SAT didn't already have enough ridiculous things on it, the Serpent came up with the funny symbol question. Here's how funny symbol questions work.

The Serpent gives you some symbol like this:

@

He tells you what it does and you're supposed to apply it. Easy. *Don't freak out* and say, "Oh, no! We never went over @ in my math class, I guess I can't do this one." The fact is that no one has ever seen that symbol in his math class. The Serpent just dreamed it up. (Yes, he loses sleep at night thinking up funny symbols and how to make them exceptionally cruel.) And he will tell you exactly what it means.

The Evil Testing Serpent defines the symbol, usually using x and y (or a and b or whatever) in terms of arithmetic commands ($+$, $-$, $\times$, $\div$), which you know how to use.

You take the numbers they give you in the question and do the arithmetic that the funny symbol represents. Be careful that you do it in the *same order* as in the definition of the funny symbol.

Okay, here are some examples:

1. If $x \diamondsuit y = x^2 + 2y$ then what is $3 \diamondsuit 4$?

   (A) $6x$

(B) 42

(C) 3

(D) 11

(E) 17

Answer: (E). Plug in 3 and 4 where x and y were in the definition.

2. $/n\backslash = 2(n^2 + n)/(n + 1)$. What is $/35\backslash$?

(A) 70

(B) 64

(C) 32

(D) $35n$

(E) 1

Answer: (A)

Note: $2(n^2 + n)/(n + 1) = 2n(n + 1)/(n + 1) = 2n$.
Take it from here.

3. $L @ K = L + {}^{K}\!/_{L}$. What is $L @ (L @ K)$?

(A) $L + 2K + {}^{K}\!/_{4}$

(B) $2L + {}^{K}\!/_{4} + 1$

(C) L

(D) $L + 1 + {}^{K}\!/_{L^2}$

(E) ${}^{L}\!/_{K}$

Okay. We know you're tired of this, so we'll give it to you:

$$L @ (L @ K) = L @ (L + {}^{K}\!/_{L})$$
$$= L + \frac{(L + {}^{K}\!/_{L})}{L}$$
$$= L + {}^{L}\!/_{L} + {}^{K}\!/_{L^2} = L + 1 + {}^{K}\!/_{L^2}$$

Answer: (D)

Remember: Always do the stuff in the parentheses first.

4.

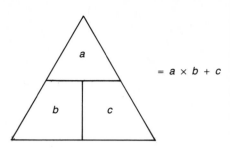

If

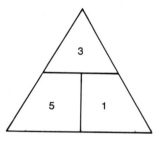 =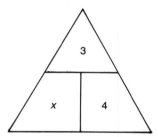

what is x?

    (A) 1½
    (B) 3
    (C) 4
    (D) 5
    (E) 8

Answer: (C)

    What else do you need to know for the math section of the SAT? Not a whole lot, actually. Many of the questions just involve common sense. Notice that in some of the questions you don't have to waste time doing mathematical computations. Sometimes the answers they have listed aren't simplified—so why in the world should you simplify yours? Look over the answers before you work yours out.

And remember, a good command of really basic things will make you work faster, and as we said earlier, speed and accuracy are essential to doing well on the math section.

Now go and take some math sections from *10 SATs*. And make your grandmother proud!

IV

TEST OF STANDARD WRITTEN ENGLISH

The ETS claims that the Test of Standard Written English (TSWE) isn't counted at all in the college admission process. With all due respect, we must say that is "El Toro Poopoo." Although the test was designed for the sole purpose of determining placement in college English courses, we have found that it does play a part in admissions decisions. Susan Murphy, the Director of Admissions and Financial Aid at Cornell University, had this to say about the TSWE: "It is designed for placement, but I suspect that in a very competitive admissions process such as we face at Cornell, a low score does trigger our faculty to ask some questions. I would say that it is a red flag. A low score would make us look carefully at a student's English Achievement scores and at the English classes that he has taken in high school. If all those things were also poor, and the essays on the application were superior, we might question whether a student wrote the essays by himself." Worth David, the Dean of Admissions at Yale, says, "Although it is certainly not one of the primary things that we look at, the TSWE score is available to the admissions officer. When candidates are in the middle of the applicant pool, we tend to bring in more and more material to aid in our decision. The TSWE score might be one of those things."

In other words, the TSWE *does* matter. We don't mean to blow its importance out of proportion; a high score on the TSWE isn't going to get you into college. A perfect score on the TSWE isn't nearly as much of a turn-on for an admissions officer as an 800 on the math or verbal section. As the above quotations indicate, it seems that it's only when your score is bad that it could become an important factor.

With this in mind, we have developed a brief review section for the TSWE. It doesn't tell you everything that you need to know to get a perfect score, but it should save you from bombing the test.

The Serpent makes this section of his SAT boring and annoying. There must be a better way to test writing skills than a test that doesn't require any writing. However, the "Clumsily Constructed Multiple Choice" method is what the Serpent uses, so you had better learn to know and love it.

TSWE questions test your ability to recognize and correct mistakes in grammar, sentence structure, and word choice. *There are no questions that directly test spelling or capitalization.* There are 50 questions on the TSWE, organized as follows:

25 usage questions
15 sentence correction questions
10 additional usage questions

The test is scored on a scale that runs from 20 to 60+. You can miss four or five questions and still get a 60+.

The best way to prepare for this moronic excuse for an exam is to take the practice tests in each edition of *10 SATs*. There are only so many grammatical rules, so the Serpent can make up only so many questions to test you on them. By practicing, you'll get used to the kind of mistakes that the Serpent plants.

In this chapter we will explain both types of TSWE questions and suggest strategies for attacking them. Then, we will cover the 11 most important grammatical rules to know for the TSWE.

THE TWO QUESTION TYPES

Type #1. Usage Questions

These questions take less time than the sentence correction questions. A typical usage question looks like this:

The <u>children</u> would <u>giggled</u> <u>as</u> they smeared applesauce
    A   B   C

<u>on each other.</u> <u>No error</u>
   D   E

You are to assume everything that isn't underlined is the way it's supposed to be, and then find the error in one of the underlined portions. The answer to the example above is (B), because *giggled* should be *giggle*.

Follow this procedure when doing usage questions:

1. Read the *whole* sentence quickly but carefully.
2. If you're positive that you see the error, mark it on the answer sheet and go on to the next problem.
3. If you don't see the error, look at each underlined portion very carefully; see if it follows the 11 rules listed later in this chapter or any other rules you might know. Something that sounds wrong probably is.
4. If you still don't find an error, mark (E).
5. If you have time left at the end of the test, go back and check all the questions for which you chose (E).

Type #2. Sentence Correction Questions

These questions take more time than the usage questions. They also play with your mind. A typical sentence correction question looks like this:

If a birth control device are going to fail, it will do so on the fourteenth day between two given periods.

(A) are going to fail, it will do so on
(B) are going to fail, it will do so about
(C) is going to fail, it will do so about
(D) is going to fail, it will do so on
(E) is going to fail, they will do so about

Your job on this type of question is to select the answer choice that would best replace the underlined part of the question. The correct answer to the above question is (D). As always, choice (A) is exactly the same as the underlined portion of the sentence and is the correct answer whenever the original sentence is okay.

This is the procedure you should follow when doing sentence correction questions:

1. Read the *whole* sentence, not just the underlined part. Often the underlined part is grammatically correct by itself but is wrong when put in the context of the whole sentence.
2. Never read choice (A). Remember, choice (A) is always

the same as the original sentence. Why read it again?

3. Even if you think that the original sentence is correct, check each one of the answer choices to see if one of them is better than the original sentence.

4. If you still think that the original sentence is cool, then pick choice (A).

5. If you think that the sentence is wrong, look for the choice that will make it right.

6. If you can't decide which is the right answer, choose the one that is phrased the most like Dan Rather would phrase it.

7. If either you can't choose between two or more answers that sound correct, or you are equally unhappy with all five answers, choose *the shortest one*. This works on an extraordinary percentage of the questions.

Strategy Note: When taking the test, do *all* the usage questions first, before doing the sentence correction questions. This is important because the usage questions take less time. Also, there is an accurate guessing technique which you should use for the sentence completion questions if you don't have time to actually solve them. (The technique is Step #7 of the above procedure. For more information about this, see Rule #7 in Section 5.)

THE 11 TSWE RULES

These are the rules most consistently tested for on the TSWE. We won't give any in-depth explanations or use any fancy grammatical terms in this section. For each rule, we will simply make you aware of the concept and then give examples. Instead of being "textbookish" and going into the grammatical theory behind our rules, we will depend on your ability to "hear" when something "sounds" right or wrong.

Nevertheless, you will have to understand the following basic grammatical terms that you probably already know. Sorry.

noun
A word that denotes a person, place, thing, idea (joy), quality (stickiness), or act (drooling).

pronoun
A word that takes the place of a noun. (Example: The Serpent is evil. *He* is cruel. *He* is a pronoun because it takes the place of *Serpent*.) *It, they, we, who,* and *them* are some examples of pronouns.

verb
A word that expresses action (jumping) or a state of being (be). They tell what's happening in the sentence.

subject
The noun that "does" the verb in the sentence. (Example: *He* drooled. *He* is the subject because *he* is the thing that drooled.)

object
The noun that the verb gets done to. (Example: He tickled *me*. *Me* is the object because *me* is the thing that got tickled.)

preposition
Prepositions are words like *to, at, in, up, over, under, after, of.* They go with objects. For example, in the phrase "in the house," *in* is a preposition and *the house* is the object.

singular
Having to do with a single thing or single unit (Example: noodle.)

plural
Having to do with more than one thing (Example: noodles.)

Rule #1. Subject-Verb Agreement Screw-ups

Subject and verb must agree in number. Isolate the subject and the verb and make sure that they match. If the subject is singular, the verb should be singular; if the subject is plural, the verb should be plural.

Example 1:
The proctor, as well as the students, were overcome by the tedious ticking of the timer and fell asleep.

Isolate: subject: proctor
           verb: were overcome

Combine: "The proctor were overcome."

This should sound wrong to you. The verb should be singular—*was overcome.* Don't be tempted by the plural word *students*; it is set off by a pair of commas, so it's not part of the subject.

Correct: The proctor, as well as the students, was overcome by the tedious ticking of the timer and fell asleep.

Three expressions that are similar to the *as well as* in the above example are: *in addition to, along with,* and *together with.* When you see one of these expressions on the TSWE, chances are the Serpent is trying to make you think that the subject is plural.

Example 2:
The anguish of the students have been a source of pleasure to the ETS.

Isolate: subject: anguish
           verb: have been

Combine: "The anguish have been a source of pleasure."

This should sound wrong to you. Don't get confused by the plural word *students,* because it isn't the subject. *Students,* in this sentence, is an object. You can tell because it comes after a preposition, *of.* Whenever a word comes after a preposition, it is an object, not a subject.

Correct: The anguish of the students has been a source of pleasure to the ETS.

Example 3:
Admissions officers at the college, although they have been instructed otherwise by the ETS, uses the TSWE scores.

Isolate: subject: Admissions officers
       verb: uses

Combine: "Admissions officers uses TSWE scores."

Admissions officers is plural, so the verb should be plural—*use.*

Correct: Admissions officers at the college, although they have been instructed otherwise by the ETS, use TSWE scores.

Note that between the subject and the verb in this sentence there are a bunch of words set-off by commas: ". . . college, although they have been instructed otherwise by ETS, uses. . ." Whenever you see a sentence like that on the SAT, a General Electric Soft Light bulb should glow radiantly in your brain. You should realize that the Serpent is putting all those words in there so that by the time you get to the verb you will have forgotten what the subject was. (See number 19 on page 47 of *10 SATs 2nd Edition.*)

Example 4:
Each of the streets were painted green.

Isolate: subject: each
       verb: were

Combine: "Each were painted green."

This one is a little trickier. You have to realize that the subject of the sentence is *each* and not *of the streets.* (*Streets* is an object of the preposition *of.*) Anytime you see "of the _____," the word that goes in the blank is an object, not a subject. Although *streets* is plural, the subject of the sentence, *Each,* is singular.

Correct: Each of the streets was painted green.

If you replace the "of the _____" part of the sentence with the word *one* it is easier to see why the subject is singular:

"Each one was painted green" sounds much better than "Each one were painted green."

There are 13 singular subjects like *each* that you should memorize: *each, every, either, neither, one, no one, everyone, everybody, someone, somebody, anyone, anybody,* and *nobody.*

Whenever you see one of these words as the subject of a sentence on the TSWE, pay careful attention to whether the verb is singular. For example:

Incorrect: Neither of the streets *were* painted green.
Correct: Neither of the streets *was* painted green.

Again, it helps to replace the "of the _____" part of the sentence with the word *one:* "Neither one was painted green" should sound better to you than "Neither one were painted green."

Incorrect: Either this street or that street *were* painted green.
Correct: Either this street or that street *was* painted green.

Incorrect: One of the streets *were* painted green.
Correct: One of the streets *was* painted green.

Rule #2: Singular Subjects Take Singular Pronouns

Singular subjects take singular pronouns; plural subjects take plural pronouns. You know the list of singular subjects that you just memorized (*each, every, either, neither, one, everyone, everybody, someone, somebody, nobody, no one, anyone,* and *anybody*)? Well, it also applies to pronouns. Whenever one of the words on the list is the subject, the pronoun that refers to that word has to be singular. This is a hard rule to "hear" because so many people break this rule that we're used to hearing the wrong way.

Example 1:
Not one of the boys read their SAT study guide.

Isolate: subject: one
pronoun: their

The above sentence doesn't sound awful to most people, but it's wrong. The subject *one* is singular, but the pronoun *their* is plural. (*Boys* is plural, but it's an object. You can tell it's an object because of the "of the _____" construction.) The correct pronoun would be *his*.

Correct: Not one of the boys read his SAT study guide.

Example 2:
Each of the girls played with their lunch.

Isolate: subject: Each
pronoun: their

Each is singular, but *their* is plural. Try replacing the *of the girls* part of the sentence with *one* and you should see why the pronoun *her* sounds better than *their*.

Correct: Each of the girls played with her lunch. (Again, think "each one.")

Rule #3: Pronoun Subjects and Objects

You must know when to use the words in the column on the left and when to use the words in the column on the right:

Subjects	Objects
I	Me
He	Him
She	Her
They	Them
We	Us
Who	Whom

The words on the left are subjects, the words on the right are objects:

I like hotdogs, but hotdogs don't like me.

He goosed Susie, so Susie kicked him.

She is good enough for Grape-Nuts, but are Grape-Nuts good enough for her?

They bit the dog, so the dog bit them.

We all hate the ETS, because the ETS hates us.

Who killed Bozo? Bozo killed whom?

Example 1:
Julio and me were down by the schoolyard.

Always simplify these sentences. Does "Me was in the schoolyard" sound right? No. "I was in the schoolyard."

Correct: Julio and I were down by the schoolyard.

Example 2:
The dog and him are eating pizza.

Does "Him is eating pizza" sound right? No. "He is eating pizza."

Correct: The dog and he are eating pizza.

Example 3:
The TSWE was easy for Huey and he because they read *Up Your Score.*

"The TSWE was easy for he" should sound wrong to you. If it doesn't sound wrong, then recognize that *he* is an object in the sentence and therefore should be *him.*

Correct: The TSWE was easy for Huey and him because they read *Up Your Score.*

Rule #4: Pronoun Consistency

Pronouns should be consistent throughout a sentence. When *one* starts with a particular pronoun, *one* should continue to use that pronoun, or a pronoun that is consistent with it, throughout *one's* whole sentence.

Example 1:

The more you study for the SAT, the more one thinks about moving to Mongolia.

This sentence starts with the pronoun *you* and then ends with the pronoun *one*. This is inconsistent. It should be either:

The more you study for the SAT, the more you think about moving to Mongolia.
or:
The more one studies for the SAT, the more one thinks about moving to Mongolia.

See numbers 8, on page 41, and 41, on page 50, of *10 SATs 2nd Edition.*

Rule #5: Correct Tense

Make sure the time of an action is consistent. Look for key "time words" such as *when, while, as, after,* and so forth, and make sure the tenses make sense.

Example 1:

After he ate the newt and brushed his teeth, I will kiss him.

The problem here is that the verbs *ate* and *brushed* happened in the past, whereas *will kiss* is going to happen in the future. Change it either to:

After he eats the newt and brushes his teeth, I will kiss him.
Or to:
After he ate the newt and brushed his teeth, I kissed him.

Example 2:
While I was painting his feet, he had tickled me.

Presumably, he *interrupted* the feet painting with his tickling, and so the sentence should read:

While I was painting his feet, he tickled me.

This makes the sentence consistent. Never mind that it's weird — consistency is all that matters on the TSWE. So, as the people in these sentences carry on with their bizarre and mildly deviant activities, just go through and make sure everything is done in the proper time sequence.

Rule #6: Adjectives and Adverbs

Remember the difference between an adjective and an adverb? If you don't, your sixth grade teacher will hunt you down and pinch you. The Evil Testing Serpent likes to mix up adverbs and adjectives.

Adjectives describe nouns. An adjective will always make grammatical sense in the phrase:
The _____ wombat. (Example: The lascivious wombat.)

Adverbs describe verbs or adjectives or other adverbs. They usually, but not always, end in "-ly." An adverb will always make grammatical sense in the sentence:
The wombat did it _____. (Example: The wombat did it lasciviously.)

Example 1:
I ran slow.

The word *slow* is an adjective. You can tell because it makes sense in the phrase, "The slow wombat." However, in Example 1, it is being used to describe the verb *ran*. This is impossible. Adjectives only describe nouns. *Adverbs* describe verbs. Use *slowly* instead.

Correct: I ran slowly.

Example 2:
Poindexter juggles good.

Poindexter has problems. The word *good* is an adjective, but it's being used to describe the word *juggles,* which is a verb. Again, you have to use the adverb:

Correct: Poindexter juggles well.

Example #3:
I hate lumpy fish on soporific afternoons.

The sentence is grammatically correct, not to mention worthy of analysis from a psychological perspective. If you immediately jumped on this sentence and tried to correct it, it means you're too tense. Eat some tofu.

Rule #7: Parallel Construction
Ideas that are parallel (related) should be expressed in the same way.

Example 1:
I like spitting, drooling, and to slurp.

Spit, drool, and slurp are parallel activities. They should be expressed in the same way:

Correct: I like spitting, drooling, and slurping.
Or: I like to spit, to drool, and to slurp.
Or: I like to spit, drool, and slurp.

Example 2:
You like spitting and drooling, but not to slurp.

Just because you don't like slurping does not mean that it shouldn't be parallel with spitting and drooling.

Correct: You like spitting and drooling, but not slurping.

Example 3:
The blender chops vegetables, squeezes oranges, and proctors can be liquefied with it.

Chopping vegetables, squeezing oranges, and liquefying proctors are all parallel actions. They should be expressed in the same way:

Correct: The blender chops vegetables, squeezes oranges, and liquefies proctors.

Rule #8: Run-On Sentences

A run-on sentence is usually two complete sentences that are incorrectly joined by a comma instead of separated by a period or a semi-colon.

Example 1:
He ate the mysterious object, it was a noodle.

This is a run-on sentence. It could be broken into two sentences:
1. He ate the mysterious object.
2. It was a noodle.

On the TSWE, however, all of the problems are one sentence long. So, leave it as one sentence and use a semi-colon.

Correct: He ate the mysterious object; it was a noodle.

Note: You only have to worry about run-ons when you're working on the sentence correction section. Usage questions don't test for run-ons.

See numbers 31 and 36 on pages 48 and 49 of *10 SATs 2nd Edition.*

Rule #9: Totally Bogus Sight Questions

These are absolutely the most ridiculous questions on the TSWE. They show how deeply and utterly absurd the Evil Testing Serpent is to have included questions this ludicrous. They don't test anything that has to do with your ability to write. They don't even test your ability to identify correct grammar. They just test whether or not you'll fail to see a single letter.

Number 9 in *10 SATs 2nd Edition* is an example of one of these noodle-headed questions.

9. Late in the war, the Germans, <u>retreating</u> <u>in haste,</u>
                                        A   B
<u>left many</u> of <u>their</u> prisoners go free. <u>No error.</u>
   C   D   E

If you didn't read the sentence carefully, you probably selected choice (E) (like Larry and Paul). Those of us who missed this question saw the word *let* where we should have seen *left*. With the word *let* the sentence is correct. With the word *left,* it is obviously wrong. In other words, we got this question wrong because we didn't see an *f*, not because we didn't know the grammar. In a sense, this question tests exactly the opposite of what it's supposed to test. People who are good writers know how the sentence is supposed to sound, so they imagine that the right word is there even when it's not. The moral of the story: *read carefully.*

Rule #10: Dangling Modifier

"Dangling modifier" is a fancy grammatical term for a simple concept. Here are some sentences with dangling modifiers.

Example 1:
Taking the test, his copy of *Up Your Score* was in his pocket.

This sentence does not mean what the person who wrote it wanted it to mean. This sentence implies that the copy of *Up Your Score* was taking the test. (This book can do many things, but it cannot take the test all by itself.) Whenever a sentence begins with a phrase like "Taking the test," which is supposed to modify (describe) a word in the sentence, the word which it modifies must be in the sentence, and it must come right after the modifying phrase.

Correct: Taking the test, he had his copy of *Up Your Score* in his pocket.

The sentence can also be corrected another way.

Correct: While he was taking the test, his copy of *Up Your Score* was in his pocket.

Dangling modifiers will be on the sentence correction section of the test. Whenever you see a sentence with an "-ing" word in a phrase at the beginning, be on the lookout for a dangling modifier.

Example 2:
Conscientious about proper grammar, dangling modifiers were always on Bertha's mind.

Were the dangling modifiers conscientious about proper grammar? No, Bertha was. So she should come right after the comma.

Correct: Conscientious about proper grammar, Bertha always had dangling modifiers on her mind.

(Example 2 is an exception to the rule about dangling modifiers having an "-ing" word at the beginning.)

Example 3:
Parachuting over the Emerald City, the ant gasped in awe.

Was the ant parachuting? Hell, yes—so the sentence is correct.

Rule #11: Sentence Logic

On the sentence correction section of the TSWE, there often are sentences that are grammatically correct but don't do a good job of saying what the writer wants them to say.

Example 1:
There often are sentences that are grammatically <u>correct, and do not say what</u> the writer wants them to say.

(A) correct, and do not say what
(B) correct, and do not say that which
(C) correct, but do not say what
(D) correct, with the exception that
(E) correct, saying not what

The correct answer is (C). One would expect that if the sentences were grammatically correct, they would say what the author wanted them to say. *But* they don't. The word *but* indicates that the part of the sentence after the comma contradicts what you would expect after reading the first part of the sentence.

Example 2:
<u>It was dark in the closet, and they</u> managed to find the exit.

(A) It was dark in the closet, and they
(B) It was dark in the closet, they
(C) It is as dark in the closet, if
(D) Although it was dark in the closet, they
(E) Until it were dark in the closet, they

The answer is (D). *Although* you would expect that in a dark closet, the exit would be hard to find, they did find the exit. The word *although* correctly conveys the author's intent that the part of the sentence after the comma should say something contrary to what one might expect after reading the first part of the sentence.

Okay—here are some pseudo-TSWE questions. There is one question for each rule and two sentences that is correct. (You caught that mistake didn't you? It should be "two sentences that *are* correct.")

PRACTICE

Usage

1. After many <u>people</u> had been <u>strangely</u> <u>painted</u> blue
             A   B   C

   and yellow, the police <u>had caught</u> the man with the
                      D

   spray can. <u>No error.</u>
              E

2. One <u>must listen</u> <u>carefully</u> to Bon Jovi's lyrics, <u>otherwise</u>
           A   B   C

   <u>you</u> might miss their thematic significance. <u>No error.</u>
   D   E

3. Confucius <u>says</u> that people <u>who</u> <u>stand</u> on the toilet <u>gets</u>
            A   B   C   D

   high on pot. <u>No error.</u>
               E

4. <u>Sagacious</u> <u>individuals</u> do not <u>construct</u> two-story <u>out-</u>
      A   B   C

   <u>houses.</u> <u>No error.</u>
   D   E

5. Every one of the <u>boys</u> in the class <u>must have</u> <u>their</u> el-
                A   B   C

   bows <u>fumigated.</u> <u>No error.</u>
        D   E

6. Bob and Joe <u>are</u> practicing <u>because</u> <u>they</u> want to defeat
            A   B   C

   Bertha and <u>she</u> in the wrestling match. <u>No error.</u>
             D   E

7. One should <u>never</u> <u>eat</u> so much sandpaper <u>that</u> you die.
      A   B   C   D

   <u>No error.</u>
     E

8. She <u>ran</u> away as <u>quick</u> as <u>she</u> could <u>from</u> the ravenous
      A   B   C   D

poodle. <u>No error.</u>
        E

9. Eggshell <u>was</u> <u>scattered</u> <u>around</u> the spot <u>where</u> Humpty
           A   B   C

Dumpty <u>felt</u> to the ground. <u>No error.</u>
       D   E

Sentence Correction

10. The most exciting thing about mushrooms is <u>their texture, a mushroom</u> is mushy and chewy.

    (A) their texture, a mushroom
    (B) their texture and mushrooms
    (C) their texture; a mushroom
    (D) their texture and that a mushroom
    (E) its texture; a mushroom

11. Bettie enjoys putting itching powder in Chip's <u>jock strap, and Chip does not</u> enjoy it.

    (A) jock strap, and Chip does not
    (B) jock strap, but Chip does not
    (C) jock strap, being not as likely that Chip will
    (D) jock strap, being as Chip will not
    (E) jock strap, and Chip does not to

12. The fish on your <u>couch, although not as smelly</u> as might be expected, are making this date unpleasant.

    (A) couch, although not as smelly
    (B) couch, but not as smelly
    (C) couch, but quite that smelly
    (D) couch, and smells
    (E) footballed! It be greenly and whom that

13. The rock star enjoyed singing obscene lyrics, break-
    ing guitars, and to make videos.

    (A) enjoyed singing obscene lyrics, breaking guitars,
        and to make videos
    (B) enjoyed singing obscene lyrics, breaking guitars,
        and to try to make videos
    (C) enjoys singing obscene lyrics, breaking guitars,
        and to make videos
    (D) enjoyed singing obscene lyrics, breaking guitars,
        and making videos
    (E) enjoyed singing obscene lyrics, breaking guitars,
        and honeys for nothing and checks for free

14. Scaling the fortress wall, the boiling oil scalded me.

    (A) wall and the boiling oil scalded me
    (B) wall, I was scalded by the boiling oil
    (C) wall, the scalding oil boiled me
    (D) wall, oil boiled and I was scalded
    (E) wall, the boiling oil sure was hot

**The correct answers to questions 1–13, and the rules that
they test, are:**
 1. D, rule 5
 2. D, rule 4
 3. D, rule 1
 4. E (sentence is correct)
 5. C, rule 2
 6. D, rule 3
 7. A, rule 4
 8. B, rule 6
 9. D, rule 9
10. C, rule 8
11. B, rule 11
12. A (sentence is correct)
13. D, rule 7
14. B, rule 10

V

GUESSING, OR THE EVIL TESTING SERPENT STRIKES BACK: ATTRACTIVE FOILS FROM HELL

Just when you thought it was safe
to go back into the testing hall...

Ome day, soon after his self-inauguration as Supreme
Commander of the High School, the ETS woke up in
his comfortable and slimy bed and realized that he was
dissatisfied with his SAT. Apparently, his torturous questions didn't always fool students. Scores were *much* higher
than he wanted them to be. He felt very sad, as well as lugubrious, melancholic, despondent, downcast, doleful,
woebegone, and disconsolate.

So, later that afternoon, he decided to pay a visit to one
of his testing halls to see what the problem was. He actually overheard a student say, "Gee, this SAT really isn't
that difficult." The Serpent felt his scales quiver in humili-
ation. Drastic action was necessary. The flaw in his SAT
had to be discovered and corrected, and fast.

The ETS knew he had made the questions as mean and
nasty as he possibly could. But after weeks of re-reading
his Slimy and Atrocious Torture and examining students
taking it, he realized what the matter was. Sometimes students would get math problems wrong and find that *their
wrong answer* wasn't one of the choices. So they tried the
problem again and got it correct the second time. At
other times, when they couldn't do one of his cruel math
or verbal questions, they would guess randomly and, out
of sheer luck, get it right. This sort of thing just wouldn't
do. But how could he possibly correct this flaw?

Then he had a brilliant idea. It was also sagacious, dis-
cerning, perspicacious, and acute. He decided to put,
within the list of answer choices, the most likely wrong
answers that students would come up with if they made
an error in answering the question or if they had to guess.
That way, if a student made a mistake or had to guess, the

student would choose one of the Serpent's wrong answers.

He decided to call these tricky wrong answer choices Attractive Foils. With this concept incorporated through-out his SAT, students would again live in fear. The Evil Testing Serpent chuckled hideously to himself and his scales shone with proud energy because he knew that his delicious years of tyranny would continue. . .forever.

Okay, don't get frightened. We didn't mean to scare anybody. Actually, the plain truth is that the Evil Testing Serpent was mistaken. He didn't plan on *Up Your Score*. We've psyched out his system of Attractive Foils and dis-covered that, if you use them properly, they actually make the SAT easier. In the following guessing section we illus-trate several techniques that we have developed to recog-nize Attractive Foils, to avoid them, and to trick the Serpent by using them to indicate the right answer.

Although we didn't call them Attractive Foils at the time, we've already discussed many types of Attractive Foils in the verbal section. For an example of a type of verbal Attractive Foil look at this antonym question from page 241 of *10 SATS 1st Edition:*

    14.   UNWITTING :   (A) intelligent
       (B) conscious   (C) disappointing
       (D) overly curious   (E) in plain sight

This is the second to last question in the sub-section so you know that it is a hard question that most students get wrong. The Serpent puts in an Attractive Foil so that stu-dents who don't know the word *unwitting* will get the ques-tion wrong. Choice (A) is the Attractive Foil in this example. The Serpent figures that students will choose (A) because they will think that *unwitting* suggests a lack of wits, as in the word *dimwit*. But *unwitting* means "uninten-tional" or "unconscious," so the correct answer is (B).

Here's another one, from page 135 of *10 SATs 1st Edition:*

10. SUFFRAGE :   (A) lack of eloquence
     (B) lack of franchise   (C) lack of pain
     (D) desire for power
     (E) desire for retribution

Choice (C) is an Attractive Foil. Students who didn't know what *suffrage* meant selected choice (C) because they thought it had something to do with "suffering." A lack of pain would be the opposite of suffering. But *suffrage* means "the right to vote." So (B) is the correct answer. *Franchise* also means "the right to vote." Eliminate Attractive Foils like these only at the end of a sub-section, where the easy answers are always wrong.

On the math section, the ETS puts in Attractive Foils that are the answers a student would get if he used the wrong method to solve a problem. He makes sure that if you screw up in the way that he hopes you will, the answer that you get with your blunder is one of the answer choices. For instance, the first question on one SAT math section (page 185 of *10 SATs 1st Edition*) reads:

1. If $x + y = 2$, then $x + y - 4 = $?
   (A) -2 (B) 0   (C) 2   (D) 4   (E) 6

The correct answer is (A), but the Serpent made sure that (C) was one of the choices in case some airhead left the minus sign out of the answer. He also made sure that (E) was there just in case some pasta brain added the 4 instead of subtracting it. He also made sure that (B) was there in case some goo-head decided that x and y were each equal to 2. So, in this example, the Attractive Foils are (B), (C), and (E).

After the following dramatic interlude that discusses the value of guessing in general, we will show you how to use Attractive Foils to your advantage.

**Guessing, the
SAT, and the
Spectre of
World
Destruction:
A Deep and
Moving Play**

The Cast:
  A sagacious guru who has read *Up Your Score*
  His naive disciple who has not

Disciple: To guess or not to guess? That is the question.
Guru: Guess, my son, guess.
Disciple: But they take off a fraction of a point for each wrong answer, whereas they don't take off any extra points if I just leave it blank. So if I guess wrong, it's going to hurt my score.
Guru: Ah, silly lad, how foolish you are. Even if you guess completely randomly, you should get a fifth of the questions correct just by the laws of chance (in the sections where there are five choices). So, the quarter of a point that the ETS takes off for each wrong answer is cancelled out on the average by the number of lucky guesses you make.
Disciple: I'm so confused. Give me an example.
Guru: I would be honored. Imagine that there were 100 questions on the test and 5 answer choices for each question. If you guess randomly you should get 20 questions correct by the laws of chance. But then the cruel SAT graders take off a quarter of a point for each of the remaining 80 questions that you missed. In other words, they'll subtract $(¼) \times 80$, or 20 points from the number of correct answers that you have. You have 20 correct answers, so you have a final score of $20 - 20 = 0$, which is exactly what you should get if you didn't know anything and were guessing randomly. It is also exactly what you would have gotten if you left everything blank. So, my child, you see that guessing didn't hurt you.
Disciple: Yeah, but it didn't help me either.
Guru: Right you are. But you were guessing randomly. If you can make educated guesses, or eliminate even one of the answer choices, then the odds will be decidedly in your favor and guessing can significantly increase your score.

Disciple: Are there any secrets to how to be a sagacious guesser like you?

Guru: It's a good thing you asked. I can recommend an incredible book that has an incredible section about guessing. It's called *Up Your Score.* It's a literary masterpiece, really. Buy some copies for your friends and family.

So, not counting that pathetic excuse for a play, just how valuable is this guessing stuff, anyway?

So valuable...We did two experiments to prove that guessing really works. First, we took the test by only looking at the answer choices without reading any of the questions. We got an average combined score of 660. Although that's not going to get anyone into Harvard, it is 260 more points than would be expected from someone with no knowledge of the questions. In our second experiment, we had 10 kids take the test and leave blank all the questions that they couldn't do. Next, we had them read this chapter and then guess on all the ones that they had left blank. Their scores were increased, by an average of 35 points, and they guessed correctly on 40 percent of the questions that they had left blank. Holy Spam! Pretty good improvement for a simple application of the 7 basic guessing rules, which are covered below.

Rule #1: One of these things is most like the others.
If you have no idea what the correct answer is, choose the one that looks the most like all the other answers. This works because the Evil Testing Serpent is going to make his Attractive Foils look as much as possible like the correct answer. Use the Attractive Foils to show you the path to the correct answer.

For example, if the answer choices are

(A) $\dfrac{\sqrt{3}}{7}$ (B) $\dfrac{\sqrt{3}}{2}$ (C) $-\dfrac{\sqrt{3}}{2}$ (D) $\dfrac{3}{2}$ (E) $5\dfrac{\sqrt{3}}{2}$

THE GUESSING TECHNIQUES

You should choose (B). Why? Because four out of five choices have a $\sqrt{3}$ in them so the correct answer probably has a $\sqrt{3}$ as well. You can eliminate choice (D). Since four out of five choices have a 2 in the denominator, the correct answer probably does too; so eliminate (A). Since four out of five answers are positive, the answer probably is too; eliminate (C). None of the answers A through D has a 5 in it, so (E) is probably wrong. This leaves (B) as the best guess.

Rule #2: Problems increase in difficulty as you go along.

We have repeatedly pointed out that each sub-section of a math or verbal section gets progressively more difficult as it goes along. The first problem in the sub-section should be easy; the last problem should be hard. This should be taken into account when you guess. If, on one of the questions near the end of a sub-section, the Evil Testing Serpent puts in an answer choice that can be arrived at through a simple calculation, that choice is probably an Attractive Foil. See page 82 of *10 SATs 1st Edition:*

25. What is the ratio of the area of a rectangle with width w and length $2w$ to the area of an isosceles right triangle with hypotenuse of length w?

(A) $\dfrac{8}{1}$ (B) $\dfrac{4}{1}$ (C) $\dfrac{2}{1}$ (D) $\dfrac{1}{2}$ (E) $\dfrac{1}{4}$

If you do not know how to do this problem, or you don't have time to do this problem, or you have a personal grudge against the word hypotenuse, you should keep in mind Rule #2. Note that this is problem number 25—the last question in the section and therefore the hardest. According to this rule, you would eliminate answers (C) and (D) because they are both simple ratios of the two numbers that are in the problem (i.e., $2w/w$, or $w/2w$). If that was all that you had to do to solve this problem, it would have been easy and therefore it wouldn't have been the last question in the section.

You could actually solve this problem by drawing the following sketch:

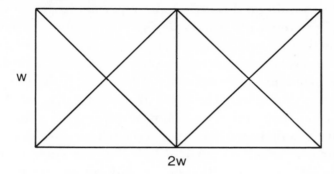

The sketch immediately shows you that 8 isosceles right triangles with hypoteneuse w fit in 1 rectangle with width w and length $2w$. In other words, the rectangle is 8 times as large as the 1 triangle. So the answer is (A).

Rule #3. Guess the middle of the range.

When the answer choices form an arithmetic progression, you should select answer choice (B), (C), or (D). What is an arithmetic progression? It's a list of numbers like 4, 5, 6, 7, 8 or 10, 20, 30, 40, 50 or 1.5, 1.4, 1.3, 1.2, 1.1. In other words, it's a bunch of numbers that get progressively larger or smaller by the same amount. 6, 9, 69, 96, 696 doesn't count as a numerical progression because although the numbers do get progressively larger, they don't do so by the same amount each time.

For example, look at this problem on page 219 of *10 SATs 1st Edition*:

7. If a rectangular sheet of paper is repeatedly folded in half until the area of the exposed side is 1/16 of the original area exposed, how many times was the paper folded?

   (A) three   (B) four   (C) five   (D) six   (E) seven

The correct answer is (B). The reason why we suggest that you guess (B), (C), or (D) in this situation is that statistics from past tests reveal that (A) or (E) is seldom the correct answer. When you think about it, it makes sense that the Serpent would do this. Remember, he wants to make sure that when you screw up, the wrong number that you get is one of the answer choices that he offers. Problems that have numerical progressions in the answers are almost always problems that involve addition, subtraction, or counting something. The most likely thing that will happen when you screw up when adding, subtracting, or counting is that you'll get an answer that's either one bigger or one smaller than it should be. For each answer choice (B), (C), and (D) there is both an answer choice that is one bigger and one that is one smaller than itself. Choice (A) doesn't have another answer choice that is one smaller than it, and choice (E) doesn't have one that is one bigger. Therefore, the Serpent would be working against himself if he made the correct answer (A) or (E). (Note: For some reason, (B) and (D) seem to show up more than (C) except on problems that ask you to find an average, in which case (C) is the best guess.)

Rule #4: Three's a crowd.

You know how you freak out when, for a couple multiple choice questions in a row, you keep getting the same letter for your answer? Well, the Serpent has been watching you and he knows this. You'd think that he would use this information to be cruel to you, and just to blow your mind he'd make all the answers for the whole test be (D). Yet he does not do this. Although it may seem that the Serpent decided to show some mercy to his victims, he knows that if nine times in a row he made choice (D) the correct answer, the students taking his SAT would panic and die from heart failure. That wouldn't be any fun for the Serpent because they could never again be subjected to his torturous exams. Nice guy, isn't he?

So, he deliberately makes sure that there aren't very many "runs." A run is 3 or more answers in a row that are the same letter. In a sample of 20 tests, there were only 9 triples (a run of length 3), whereas statistically there should have been about 24. Also, there were no runs of 4 or more and there should have been about 9.

So if you pick (C) for 2 questions in a row that you think you got right, and you're not sure about the next one, don't guess (C). This rule should also be applied if, for instance, you chose (D) on question 15, skipped question 16, and then chose (D) again on question 17. When you go back to guess at number 16, don't guess (D).

Note: If somewhere in the test your answers form a triple but you are confident that they are correct, don't change them just because of this rule. It might, however, be wise to pay special attention to those questions if you have time to recheck your answers.

Rule #5: Multiple true-false method.

This rule pertains to a type of question that comes up occasionally in math and reading comprehension questions in the following nasty format:

Based upon what you read in the passage, which is true?
  I.   The Beastie Boys contribute in many ways to modern society.
  II. A watched pot boils eventually.
  III. Jim Morrison is alive and living in the body of Dr. Ruth.

(A) I only
(B) II only
(C) I and II only
(D) I and III only
(E) I, II, and III

According to Rule #5, in this example you would pick an answer that has a I in it because I shows up four times in the answer choices whereas II only shows up three times and III only twice. This works because, if indeed I is true, the Serpent considers any answer with a I in it to be an Attractive Foil. If you have no idea at all about whether the other statements are true, select *I only*. However, if you have a hunch that statement II is correct as well, then you would go with (C) because that contains both I (which shows up the most) and II, which you think might be correct.

Sometimes there is a tie between two numbers. If the answer choices had been

(A) I only
(B) II only
(C) III only
(D) I and III only
(E) I, II, and III

then there would have been three occurrences of I and three occurrences of III. In this situation, you should pick an answer that has both I and III in it, so you would choose either (D), if you think that statement II is wrong, or (E) if you think that II might be correct.

Rule #6: Pick "non-answers" at the beginning, not at the end.

On the math section, there will always be a few questions that have as an answer choice, "It cannot be determined from the information given." *The Princeton Review* has devised a good rule for guessing on this type of question. They say that if "It cannot be determined..." is offered at the *beginning* of either math section (one of the first 19 questions on the 25 question math section, or one of the first 7 on the 35 question math section), then it has about a 50 percent chance of being correct. However, if it is offered near the *end* of the test, it's probably wrong.

Why does this work? Well, the Evil Testing Serpent knows that most students will not be able to do the last couple of questions. He wants to make sure that there is a tempting answer choice for those students. So he makes one of them "It cannot be determined from the information given." Many students are conned into selecting this sort of answer at the end, when the problems are hard, because they are usually rushed for time and don't see a solution to the problem right away, even though there is one. In other words, when a "non-answer" is offered near the end of a section, it's probably a trick.

Note: There is no evidence to the effect that Rule #6 works on the usage questions on the TSWE (the questions where you pick the part of the sentence that's screwed up). In other words don't avoid choice (E), "No error," just because it is a non-answer. In fact, if you have to guess, it usually suggests that you can't find anything wrong with the sentence, so the sentence is probably correct and (E) is the answer.

Rule #7: On the Test of Standard Written English, select a short answer.

English is a relatively efficient language. Good writing often involves short, to–the–point sentences that don't go on for ever and ever talking about all sorts of things, and getting redundant, and being just generally too long, when they could be short but aren't because they're long, in fact much longer than they have to be (like this sentence). For this reason, the shortest answer on the sentence correction section of the TSWE is generally the best guess. Take a look at number 38 in the TSWE that is provided on page 49 of *10 SATs 2nd Edition:*

38. Mr. Howe's class has organized a special program for our <u>school: the purpose being to</u> help us increase our understanding of Japanese culture.

(A) school: the purpose being to
(B) school and the purpose is to
(C) school, the purpose is to
(D) school, being to
(E) school to

The correct answer is (E). It is the shortest answer. Using this method on the sample test in *10 SATs 2nd Edition,* you would have been correct on *10 out of 15* sentence correction questions. If you had guessed wildly you would expect to have gotten only 3 questions correct.

A FINAL AND IMPORTANT LAST WORD CONCERNING GUESSING

Before we move on to the next section, you should know that guessing on a question is really no substitute for knowing the answer. Formally, we call this the Sponge Brain Rule, which says: "If you know the right answer, don't guess a different answer."

VI

BUT WAIT!
YOU ALSO
GET...

"A man walks down the street
Says, 'Why am I short of attention?
Got a short little span of attention
But, oh, my nights are so long.' " — Paul Simon

CONCENTRA-TION

Your *concentration span* is the length of time that you can direct your attention to a given task without spacing out. Every task also has what is called a *distraction potential*. The higher the distraction potential of a given task, the more difficult it is for you to apply your concentration span. We all know that the distraction potential of the SAT can be very high indeed. Not only is the test itself difficult and boring, but the test hall atmosphere, complete with creaking chairs, strange odors, ticking watches, sneezing people, and shuffling papers can add to the distraction.

Imagine the following scenario. It's two hours into the test. You're on the second math section, and you get to this question:

14. If $a * b = 2ab$ and $a \dagger b = ab/2$ then what is the value of $a * (b \dagger c)$?

   (A) $4ab$
   (B) $4bc$
   (C) $2abc$
   (D) abc
   (E) ac

This is not too hard a problem to do when you're fresh, but after two hours it can be tricky. If someone were to take a "brain transcript" of you trying to do this problem, here's what it might look like:

"Okay, it's one of those dopey problems with the funny symbol thingies. Let's see, what's the deal? . . . Oh, I got it. You stick in the jigger bobby for $b \dagger c$ which makes $ab/2$, then . . . no, no, no, crap, it's $bc/2$ that you plug in. Then that leaves $a * (bc/2)$. How much more time do I have left?

Twelve minutes. That's 2/5 of the time for this section and I have more than 2/5 of the questions to do. Oh no, I'm behind. Okay, okay, okay. Where was I? Oh yeah, you stick in $2a$ which makes $2abc/2$ and then I wish this idiot would stop tapping his foot. Tap. Tap. Tap. Tap. There he goes again. His hair is slimy. I wonder where he's applying to college. Tap. Tap. Why doesn't he wash his hair? Gross! Okay, okay, okay. $2abc/2 = abc$ which is answer (D). Good. Fill in (D)."

Well, you got the question right, but only after much wasted thought. The worst mistake was checking the time. Never do this in the middle of a problem, only between problems. And never let the slightest distraction bother you—foot tapping, slimy hair, or whatever. Of course, this is much easier said than done. It's not as simple as just deciding that you are going to start to concentrate. Simply deciding to concentrate can leave you with a brain transcript that looks like this:

"Concentrate. Concentrate, damn it. Okay. I'm just gonna focus my brain like you wouldn't believe. This is the most important three hours of my life and I am going to concentrate intensely for the whole time. Ooooh, I'm really concentrating now. His slimy hair isn't bothering me a bit. This is total concentration—no distractions. The tap tap tap noise that his foot is making right now, which I wish he would stop, isn't bothering me either. You could stick me with pins and I wouldn't feel it. Okay, what problem am I on?..."

You're concentrating so hard on concentrating that you're not concentrating on the test. The trick is to learn to concentrate without thinking about concentrating. Your mind should be effortlessly focused. You should feel like you are meditating. To learn to do this you must practice. Training your brain is just like training any other part of your body—you have to exercise it.

Concentration exercises are usually pretty dopey. They're the kind of thing that you read about, say to yourself, "That's dopey," and move on without even trying them once. Typical concentration exercises are things like running through the multiplication table in your head and trying not to space out. Any mental task that can be done for 20 consecutive minutes, but which is tedious enough that your brain would be tempted to space out, makes for a good concentration exercise.

We have discovered that drinking games make excellent concentration exercises. If you practice these games for 20 minutes a day for a month, you will find that your concentration span will improve dramatically. You will also be admired when you go to parties at college because you will be so good at these games.

Important Note: Usually these games are played in groups, and whenever someone screws up, that person has to take a drink. You, however, should play them alone and without doing the drinking. You will kill the whole value of the concentration game if you stop every few minutes to drink. You will also kill off so many brain cells after a month of these games that you will have no brain left with which to concentrate.

We've provided you with guidelines for two drinking games. We suggest that you play Game #1 for 10 minutes followed by Game #2 for 10 minutes. It is good practice to try to do these games with the television on to see if you can concentrate so intensely that you are not even aware the TV is on.

GAME #1: KERPLUNK!

This one starts off simply but gets difficult. Say to yourself, *in a steady rhythm*, the following sequence of sentences:

1. One frog—two eyes—four legs—in a pond—kerplunk!

Then multiply everything by two:

2. Two frogs—four eyes—eight legs—in a pond— kerplunk! kerplunk!

Then you do it with three frogs:

3. Three frogs—six eyes—twelve legs—in a pond—kerplunk! kerplunk! kerplunk!

As you can see, the basic pattern is:

X. X frogs—two X eyes—four X legs—in a pond—repeat "kerplunk" X times

Keep doing the sequence. Whenever you say something wrong (i.e., 12 legs when you should have said 16 legs, or forgetting to say "in a pond," or not knowing how many times you have said "kerplunk," or forgetting which number is next) or whenever you lose the mental rhythm and have to pause to think of what to say next, you have to divide the number of frogs that you are on by two and then start again. For example, if you were on 10 frogs and you said that they had 40 eyes, you would have to go back to "5 frogs—10 eyes—20 legs—in a pond. . ."

GAME #2: BUZZ

This is a counting game. Pick a number between 2 and 10, not counting 2 and 10. Then start counting *in a steady rhythm*. Whenever you come to a number that is:

1. a multiple of the number, or,
2. has the number as one of its digits

you don't say the number but instead you say, "Buzz." The best way to explain this is to do an example:

Suppose the number is 4, then you count:

1, 2, 3, buzz, 5, 6, 7, buzz, 9, 10, 11, buzz, 13, buzz, 15, buzz, 17, 18, 19. . .

If you miss a "buzz" or lose the rhythm, you have to go back to the number that is half of the number that you screwed up on.

GAME #3: SAT PRACTICE TESTS

This game has not gained widespread popularity in bars, but it is the most useful concentration game. If you take a lot of practice tests and really practice concentrating on each section for the entire half hour, you will concentrate better on the real test, too.

MOVING ON

Another concentration problem you might have is an inability to move right on to the next question if you have not been able to solve the previous one. This difficulty arises because your mind is unwilling to accept that it is unable to do the problem and wants to keep working on it. A brain transcript of this might look like:

Old Problem

"Okay, screw this. Too difficult. Can't figure it out."

"But wait! I can do this one. If I just knew what this part was. I've already spent two minutes on it. I might as well finish it. No. That's stupid. Move on to the next question."

"Hey, maybe choice (D) is also right on this problem. No, that can't be right. Move on to the next problem."

New Problem

NOT LOOKED AT YET

"This one looks easy. I can do this one. Choice (D) looks good but. . ."

"Where was I? Oh yeah. Choice (D) looks good."

"Okay, it was (D). I'll fill that in on the answer sheet."

This sort of zigzagging really wastes time. When your brain tries to occupy itself with two problems at the same time, it doesn't work well on either of the problems. You have to trick your subconscious mind so that it will move on to the next problem without trying to go back. The three things that will help you do this are:
1. Guess—This is another good reason for guessing on all

questions that you can't answer. When you guess, your subconscious is satisfied that it has found an answer and is more willing to move on.

2. You shall return—Tell your brain that you're going to come back to the problem after you've finished the test. Then your brain will be more willing to leave the problem temporarily.

3. Practice—The more timed practice tests you take, the more relaxed your brain will become with moving on.

PROCTORS: MINDLESS SLAVES OF THE ETS

Profile
Proctors come in three sizes. The first and most prestigious model is the test center supervisor—a popular item but available only in limited quantities. The TCS is, in short, the Big Cheese—she's in charge of the whole test center. She's supposed to find all of the underling proctors, procure rooms, and maintain contact with ETS.

The next sized proctor is the supervisor, who's the bigshot in each room. The supervisor is the dude

The Greek word *proktos* means "anus." So does the English word *proctor*. SAT proctors tend to be haphazardly selected, and for the most part they do not give a flying poo about your life or your problems. They're only paid a pittance, not enough to make them care.

Sure we're being harsh, but we've interviewed students at many schools and we have heard some nasty horror stories about incompetent and ignorant proctors. On each test date, students across the nation go in to take the SAT in what they hope will be a fair environment. Instead, some of them must cope with bumbling idiots who forget to read instructions, eliminate break time, talk while you work, or give incorrect responses to student questions (responses like, "No, you shouldn't guess."). Many proctors simply haven't learned how to do their job. They are given a proctor's manual with specific instructions on what forms of ID are acceptable, how far apart to seat people, what to do if there's a fire alarm, etc. But since their wages are not incentive enough for them to read it and no one ever checks on them, they usually are left to say and do whatever they want. Here, once again, we discover the Evil Testing Serpent doing his foul work. He insidiously fails to insist on the quality of the proctors he selects.

If you happen to get good proctors, thank them, kiss them, and offer to nibble gently on their earlobes. (They'll love this.) However, you should be prepared for a bad one and know how to cope. This will save you from getting screwed.

To be on guard against a bad proctor, you must, to quote The Clash, "Know Your Rights." Your liberties so generously granted to you by the ETS include the following:

1. You have the right to 30 *silent* minutes to work on each section. The 30 minutes begin *after* the proctor has finished reading all instructions, and not before!
2. You have the right to a five- to ten-minute break at the end of each hour.
3. You have the right to use the test booklet as scrap paper.
4. You have the right to have your seat changed if you give a legitimate reason. The proctor, of course, decides whether your reason is "legitimate" or not. Being placed in a right-handed desk when you are left–handed, having the sun in your eyes, and sitting with water dripping on your head from a leak in the ceiling are all examples of legitimate reasons.
5. You have the right to breathe.

If any of these rights are violated, *speak up*. If one of the proctors says something you think is questionable or even admits that he doesn't know something, go ask the supervisor, who we can only *hope* knows what she's doing. Never be afraid of "authorities" who actually know less than you do about their own jobs. Be polite, but insist. Remember, it's your future, and you don't want to spend it as an SAT proctor, do you?

In order to succeed on the SAT, it is most important to use your *mind*. If you arrive at the testing area without your *mind*, you are sure to do poorly on the test. (There have been reports of test-takers in California who scored above 600 without their minds; these rumors have been investigated and have been found to be vicious hoaxes.) Most of this book is devoted to training the mind to meet

who reads the directions in a clear and carefully modulated voice ("Please read the directions as I read them aloud to you . . ."). The supervisor is in charge of all the proctors in his room.

The actual proctors are the people who hand out the tests and answer sheets and make sure that you don't cheat.

Proctors are selected by the test center. Often local teachers are chosen as proctors— people whose faces are familiar to students. They are paid by ETS. Supervisors are paid in proportion to the number of students taking the test and proctors are paid a flat fee.

YOGA AND THE SAT

THE SAT: A Body-Oriented Experience

the intellectual challenge that the SAT presents. However, a certain amount of physical conditioning is necessary as well. Each year thousands of students all across the nation suffer from muscle fatigue, leg cramps, and spinal curvature as a direct result of the SAT. Yes, the SAT can be a grueling, bone-breaking, lung-collapsing experience for the ill-prepared. How can this be? How can taking a test be so physically draining? Simply stated, all the misery is caused by this little beastie:

And well you should gasp! This demented version of a chair, or one like it, will be your home during the three most important hours of your high school career. Equipped with ample desk space of about one square foot, this chair undoubtedly will have you making a fool of yourself as you attempt to keep your test booklet and answer sheet together on the desk and not let them fall all over the floor. They will fall on the floor anyway, making a rustling sound, and you will wind up annoying everyone in the testing hall. If you are left-handed, the situation will be even worse—you will wind up with the book on your lap and the answer sheet on the desk—leaving your left hand wrapped across your body to mark the circles. This is misery. Demand from the proctor a more appropriate place to take the test. He will probably just laugh wickedly and enjoy watching you suffer.

To make matters worse, the legs of the chair are usually too short and the edges too sharp. If you're not careful, you'll cut yourself and there'll be blood everywhere. And if you don't keep your posture (practically impossible to maintain), you'll wind up in traction with a slipped disc. Only the strong survive.

But there is hope. For help, we suggest you turn to knowledge that has existed for centuries in the eastern regions of the world. The ancient art of yoga, we have found, offers the most relevant conditioning for the serious-minded. If you practice the following exercise, starting at least a month before the test, you will suffer minimal discomfort from your immediate surroundings during the test.

Cheating is rampant at many test centers. Among the cheating methods we have encountered are: sharing answers during the breaks between sections, peeking at other people's answer sheets, using calculator watches, communicating answers through sophisticated body language codes, leaving a dictionary in the bathroom and looking up words during the breaks, and even having one student take the test for another student.

CHEATING

Two kids with whom we went to high school cheated by using the following method. Since their last names were Basset and Bates (the names have been changed to protect the guilty) they knew that they would be sitting next to each other during the test. Basset was a math whiz and Bates was a vocabulary guru. So Basset did both of his own math sections while Bates did both of his own verbal sections. When the proctor turned around, they traded tests. Basset did Bates's math sections and Bates did Basset's verbal sections. They both did very well and—what a surprise—they both got exactly the same score.

Should you cheat? *No. You should not cheat.* You see, there's nothing wrong with beating the system by learning what you've learned in this book because, although we do teach you a lot of tricks, we don't break any rules. But if you beat the system by breaking the rules, you are doing something that's wrong. You will feel guilty and wish you hadn't done it. When your friends who didn't cheat don't get into their first choice colleges and you do, you will feel awful. Just ask Basset and Bates.

So why did we write this section? To make you aware that cheating is a reality and that you shouldn't let people cheat off you. In fact, you should screw them over when they try. Suppose that during the break someone asks you what you got for number 22. Even though you know that the answer is (B), tell them that you got (C) and you're totally sure that you got it right. Then after the test say to that person, "Did I tell you (C)? I meant to say (B). Golly, I'm really sorry."

A Gray Area

Cheating by getting answers from other people is clearly wrong. The most common form of cheating, however, does not involve getting answers from others. The most common method of cheating is working on sections of the test after the 30 minutes allotted for that section are over. At the bottom of every section the Evil Testing Serpent warns you in big, bold, letters:

STOP

IF YOU FINISH BEFORE TIME IS CALLED, YOU MAY CHECK YOUR WORK ON THIS SECTION ONLY. DO NOT WORK ON ANY OTHER SECTION.

At many test centers, no one checks what section you are on. We would estimate that about half the kids at our test center cheated by using this method. The three of us were good boys and didn't. But after the test when we realized how many of our friends had done this, we felt like we were at an unfair disadvantage for not having done it.

Clearly, this kind of cheating is not as bad as getting answers from other people. It could be argued that when your future is in the balance, it's not so bad to borrow a minute from the math section to work on the verbal section that you didn't quite finish, especially if half your classmates are doing it. On the other hand, it's still cheating and if you do it you are screwing over the honest people who won't do as well as you because they didn't cheat. This is a gray area. It's a question of personal ethics—either you have them by now or you don't.

Robert Southey, the author of *The Three Bears* and arguably the worst poet ever, once said, "The desert circle spreads like the round ocean." He was referring, of course, to the metaphorical relationship between circles and the SAT. Circles are important. Everyone always says that to get an 800, 800 you have to work really hard and be a brain. Actually, all you have to do is put eight circles together in the correct pattern. (Can you find the eight circles? Sure you can.)

Circles are also quite significant in that there are 180 of them that you will have to fill in during the course of the test. This is about how to fill in those little circles. (Actually, they're not really circles, they're ovals.)

LITTLE CIRCLES

Undoubtedly, you've had to fill in lots of little circles in your life. You probably never gave much thought to technique or speed. In fact, as far as we know, no one in modern science has ever researched the science of filling in circles. We are the first ones. We'll probably win the Nobel Prize.

In the course of our research, we have discovered that some students spend as much as 2.3 seconds per circle. At that rate, they will spend 7 minutes and 4 seconds of their total testing time filling in circles. On the other hand, those students who master this chapter will spend only 0.4 seconds per circle and will therefore spend only 1 minute and 12 seconds filling them all in. That's almost 6 extra minutes that can be spent working on the test.

We consulted with Dr. Elizabeth Berger to develop an anatomically correct description of the technique that we believe to be most efficient:

> Grasp your number 2 pencil between the distal closed space of terminal phalanx II and the palmar surface of the corresponding area of the distal phalanx of the pollicis. Additional support is derived from the radial border of the distal interphalangeal joint of the third phalange of the upper extremity. The flexor pollicis brevis, which is innervated by the median and deep ulnar nerves and is in close proximity to the princeps pollicis artery, assists in this action as do the tendons of the flexor, the digiti superficialis and those of the flexor digiti profundis. (Certainly, the ulnar surface of the upper extremity distal to the olecranon process may rest upon the writing surface *provided that* the flexor carpi ulnaris, flexor carpi radialis, and the palmaris longus maintain a tonic contraction.)
>
> The abductor pollicis brevis, which originates from the flexor retinaculum, the tuberosity of the scaphoid and the trapezium, and the exten-

sor pollicis longus engage in antagonistic move-
ments with the flexor pollicis brevis and the
abductor pollicis obliquus, assisted by the first
and second lumbricales which insert upon the
tendon of the extensor digiti communis.

Got that? In other words, use a circular motion that
works from the inside to the outside. Time trials and
super-slo-mo analysis have proven that the most efficient
method is:

The In-to-Out Circle Method

Common mistakes made by high school students who
are not familiar with our ground-breaking research
include:

The Vertical Lines Method

The Horizontal Lines Method

The Out-to-In Circle Method

The Moron Dot Method

To perfect your technique follow the rules below:

1. Don't be compulsive about filling in every nook and cranny. Just make sure that in one swift movement, at least 90% of the circle is filled in. Make it black, but just don't waste time going over it twice to make it black again.

   If you don't fill in each circle perfectly, you can fill them in more thoroughly during one of the breaks between tests. Just take care not to waste time during the test.

2. Leave the point of one of your pencils *dull.* Although you don't want to use a dull pencil on the math section (you want a good pencil for scratch work) it will save you time on the verbal and TSWE section because the more surface area the point of your pencil has, the fewer strokes you need to make to fill in the circle.

3. Although you don't want your arm to be too stiff, you should press hard on the answer sheet. The darker the mark, the more likely the scanner is to see it. This is an important factor if you're not filling in your circles all the way.

4. Practice, practice, practice. Try to get your time below 0.5 seconds per circle. The following pages are filled with 800 (our favorite number) circles for you to practice on. If you get your time below 0.3 seconds, you may be able to qualify for the *Olympics.*

Ⓐ Ⓑ Ⓒ Ⓓ Ⓔ   Ⓐ Ⓑ Ⓒ Ⓓ Ⓔ   Ⓐ Ⓑ Ⓒ Ⓓ Ⓔ
Ⓐ Ⓑ Ⓒ Ⓓ Ⓔ   Ⓐ Ⓑ Ⓒ Ⓓ Ⓔ   Ⓐ Ⓑ Ⓒ Ⓓ Ⓔ
Ⓐ Ⓑ Ⓒ Ⓓ Ⓔ   Ⓐ Ⓑ Ⓒ Ⓓ Ⓔ   Ⓐ Ⓑ Ⓒ Ⓓ Ⓔ
Ⓐ Ⓑ Ⓒ Ⓓ Ⓔ   Ⓐ Ⓑ Ⓒ Ⓓ Ⓔ   Ⓐ Ⓑ Ⓒ Ⓓ Ⓔ
Ⓐ Ⓑ Ⓒ Ⓓ Ⓔ   Ⓐ Ⓑ Ⓒ Ⓓ Ⓔ   Ⓐ Ⓑ Ⓒ Ⓓ Ⓔ
Ⓐ Ⓑ Ⓒ Ⓓ Ⓔ   Ⓐ Ⓑ Ⓒ Ⓓ Ⓔ   Ⓐ Ⓑ Ⓒ Ⓓ Ⓔ
Ⓐ Ⓑ Ⓒ Ⓓ Ⓔ   Ⓐ Ⓑ Ⓒ Ⓓ Ⓔ   Ⓐ Ⓑ Ⓒ Ⓓ Ⓔ
Ⓐ Ⓑ Ⓒ Ⓓ Ⓔ   Ⓐ Ⓑ Ⓒ Ⓓ Ⓔ   Ⓐ Ⓑ Ⓒ Ⓓ Ⓔ
Ⓐ Ⓑ Ⓒ Ⓓ Ⓔ   Ⓐ Ⓑ Ⓒ Ⓓ Ⓔ   Ⓐ Ⓑ Ⓒ Ⓓ Ⓔ
Ⓐ Ⓑ Ⓒ Ⓓ Ⓔ   Ⓐ Ⓑ Ⓒ Ⓓ Ⓔ   Ⓐ Ⓑ Ⓒ Ⓓ Ⓔ
Ⓐ Ⓑ Ⓒ Ⓓ Ⓔ   Ⓐ Ⓑ Ⓒ Ⓓ Ⓔ   Ⓐ Ⓑ Ⓒ Ⓓ Ⓔ
Ⓐ Ⓑ Ⓒ Ⓓ Ⓔ   Ⓐ Ⓑ Ⓒ Ⓓ Ⓔ   Ⓐ Ⓑ Ⓒ Ⓓ Ⓔ
Ⓐ Ⓑ Ⓒ Ⓓ Ⓔ   Ⓐ Ⓑ Ⓒ Ⓓ Ⓔ   Ⓐ Ⓑ Ⓒ Ⓓ Ⓔ
Ⓐ Ⓑ Ⓒ Ⓓ Ⓔ   Ⓐ Ⓑ Ⓒ Ⓓ Ⓔ   Ⓐ Ⓑ Ⓒ Ⓓ Ⓔ
Ⓐ Ⓑ Ⓒ Ⓓ Ⓔ   Ⓐ Ⓑ Ⓒ Ⓓ Ⓔ   Ⓐ Ⓑ Ⓒ Ⓓ Ⓔ
Ⓐ Ⓑ Ⓒ Ⓓ Ⓔ   Ⓐ Ⓑ Ⓒ Ⓓ Ⓔ   Ⓐ Ⓑ Ⓒ Ⓓ Ⓔ

(A) (B) (C) (D) (E)   (A) (B) (C) (D) (E)   (A) (B) (C) (D) (E)
(A) (B) (C) (D) (E)   (A) (B) (C) (D) (E)   (A) (B) (C) (D) (E)
(A) (B) (C) (D) (E)   (A) (B) (C) (D) (E)   (A) (B) (C) (D) (E)
(A) (B) (C) (D) (E)   (A) (B) (C) (D) (E)   (A) (B) (C) (D) (E)
(A) (B) (C) (D) (E)   (A) (B) (C) (D) (E)   (A) (B) (C) (D) (E)
(A) (B) (C) (D) (E)   (A) (B) (C) (D) (E)   (A) (B) (C) (D) (E)
(A) (B) (C) (D) (E)   (A) (B) (C) (D) (E)   (A) (B) (C) (D) (E)
(A) (B) (C) (D) (E)   (A) (B) (C) (D) (E)   (A) (B) (C) (D) (E)
(A) (B) (C) (D) (E)   (A) (B) (C) (D) (E)   (A) (B) (C) (D) (E)
(A) (B) (C) (D) (E)   (A) (B) (C) (D) (E)   (A) (B) (C) (D) (E)
(A) (B) (C) (D) (E)   (A) (B) (C) (D) (E)   (A) (B) (C) (D) (E)
(A) (B) (C) (D) (E)   (A) (B) (C) (D) (E)   (A) (B) (C) (D) (E)
(A) (B) (C) (D) (E)   (A) (B) (C) (D) (E)   (A) (B) (C) (D) (E)
(A) (B) (C) (D) (E)   (A) (B) (C) (D) (E)   (A) (B) (C) (D) (E)
(A) (B) (C) (D) (E)   (A) (B) (C) (D) (E)   (A) (B) (C) (D) (E)
(A) (B) (C) (D) (E)   (A) (B) (C) (D) (E)   (A) (B) (C) (D) (E)
(A) (B) (C) (D) (E)   (A) (B) (C) (D) (E)   (A) (B) (C) (D) (E)
(A) (B) (C) (D) (E)   (A) (B) (C) (D) (E)   (A) (B) (C) (D) (E)
(A) (B) (C) (D) (E)   (A) (B) (C) (D) (E)   (A) (B) (C) (D) (E)
(A) (B) (C) (D) (E)   (A) (B) (C) (D) (E)   (A) (B) (C) (D) (E)
(A) (B) (C) (D) (E)   (A) (B) (C) (D) (E)   (A) (B) (C) (D) (E)
(A) (B) (C) (D) (E)   (A) (B) (C) (D) (E)   (A) (B) (C) (D) (E)
(A) (B) (C) (D) (E)   (A) (B) (C) (D) (E)   (A) (B) (C) (D) (E)
(A) (B) (C) (D) (E)   (A) (B) (C) (D) (E)   (A) (B) (C) (D) (E)
(A) (B) (C) (D) (E)   (A) (B) (C) (D) (E)   (A) (B) (C) (D) (E)
(A) (B) (C) (D) (E)   (A) (B) (C) (D) (E)   (A) (B) (C) (D) (E)
(A) (B) (C) (D) (E)   (A) (B) (C) (D) (E)   (A) (B) (C) (D) (E)
(A) (B) (C) (D) (E)   (A) (B) (C) (D) (E)   (A) (B) (C) (D) (E)
(A) (B) (C) (D) (E)   (A) (B) (C) (D) (E)   (A) (B) (C) (D) (E)
(A) (B) (C) (D) (E)   (A) (B) (C) (D) (E)   (A) (B) (C) (D) (E)
(A) (B) (C) (D) (E)   (A) (B) (C) (D) (E)   (A) (B) (C) (D) (E)
(A) (B) (C) (D) (E)   (A) (B) (C) (D) (E)   (A) (B) (C) (D) (E)
(A) (B) (C) (D) (E)   (A) (B) (C) (D) (E)   (A) (B) (C) (D) (E)
(A) (B) (C) (D) (E)   (A) (B) (C) (D) (E)   (A) (B) (C) (D) (E)
(A) (B) (C) (D) (E)   (A) (B) (C) (D) (E)   (A) (B) (C) (D) (E)
(A) (B) (C) (D) (E)   (A) (B) (C) (D) (E)   (A) (B) (C) (D) (E)
(A) (B) (C) (D) (E)

ARE THE SATs SEXIST?

The SAT is supposed to be an indicator of how well students are apt to do in college. According to the article "Are the SATs Unfair to Women?" in the November 1986 issue of *Glamour* magazine, in 1985, the average combined score for women was 59 points lower than the average score for men. So one might deduce that women must do worse in college than men. However, women, on the average, get better grades in high school and college than men do. If the SAT is supposed to predict freshman grades, then women should be outscoring men by 10 points on the SAT.

If men were scoring 59 points higher solely because they were doing better on the math section, it would not necessarily indicate a flaw in the test. Numerous studies have demonstrated that men generally are better math students than are women. But men are also scoring an average of 10 to 12 points better on the verbal section, despite the fact that many other standardized tests indicate that women are superior at verbal skills. Something is clearly wrong here.

Some people argue that these statistics are not indicative of a flaw in the test. They claim that women do better than men in college because they take easier courses. Others argue that these SATistics indicate that the SAT is a sexist test. They claim that the majority of the people who make up the questions are male and that verbal questions deal more with scientific subjects than they did twenty years ago when women scored higher than men. They cite SAT questions like this as an example of how the SAT is sexist:

DECOY : DUCK ::

(A) net : butterfly
(B) web : spider
(C) lure : fish
(The article skips D and E.)

Women missed this question more than they should have statistically. This could be because it concerns hunting, which more men do than women.

CANCELLING COUNSELING

If, after the test, you feel like you might have screwed up, it's only natural and you shouldn't worry about it. However, if you *know* that you screwed up, you should cancel your scores. If you made some grievous error like choosing words that were synonyms when you were supposed to be doing antonyms, or falling asleep during a section, then it is probably wise to cancel. But don't cancel just because you made a few stupid mistakes.

The simplest way to cancel is to fill out a Test Cancellation Form before you leave the test center. However, if you decide to cancel after you've left the test, you must notify the ETS by the Wednesday after the Saturday that you take the test. (For details, refer to your SAT Student Bulletin.)

Dweebs who want amazing scores memorize all the problems that they weren't sure about and then go home and see if they guessed correctly. If they did guess correctly, they keep their scores. Otherwise, they cancel.

If you cancel, your score report will read "Absent or Scores Delayed."

THE SSS AND THE SDQ

With his spare time, the Evil Testing Serpent likes to play matchmaker. This is why he invented the Student Search Service (SSS). The SSS is like a computer dating service, except that instead of matching sexually frustrated singles, it matches colleges with potential students. It's free, and it's a good way to get lots of mail, so you might as well do it.

In order to enroll in the program, you have to fill out the Student Descriptive Questionnaire (SDQ) in the Student Bulletin for either the SAT or the PSAT (both of which are available in your high school guidance office). By the way, doing this questionnaire is a great opportunity to practice filling in little circles.

Unless you're a compulsively ethical person, there is no reason why you have to tell the truth when answering the questionnaire. If you have no artistic ability, but you still want to see the pretty pictures in the brochures that the art schools send out, then fill out question 6 to say that you got "A or Excellent in Art and Music." Also, do not be modest when answering the questionnaire. If you're good at something, say that you're great at it. That way you'll be sure to get mail from the colleges that are interested in that skill. The way it works is the colleges send ETS a list of characteristics that they are looking for in their students, and the ETS sends them only the name, address, sex, date of birth, social security number, high school, and intended major of students who match those characteristics. The college doesn't know your answers to individual questions; it only knows that the match-making Serpent thought you might be compatible.

Another similarity between the SSS and a dating service is that they both make mistakes, matching you up with some real losers. The Registration Bulletin claims that you will get mail only from schools with "the academic programs and other features you find important." This is false. If you put on the questionnaire that you are an Alaskan native who wants to study philosophy and has no mechanical ability, you will still get mail from the Mormon School of Interplanetary Auto Mechanics.

FOOD SMUGGLING

The ETS says that food is strictly prohibited in the test center. Forget that. If you're going to be hungry, or you want an extra bit of energy, bring some food with you.

You shouldn't eat the food during the test because that would waste valuable time. Instead, snack between sections. Choosing your SAT menu can be lots of fun. Here are a few guidelines and suggestions.
1. Nothing noisy: no potato chips, carrots, rice cakes, or tuna casseroles (at least not the kind with Cornflakes on top)
2. Nothing sticky: no cookie batter, maple syrup, toffee, or Superglue
3. Nothing big: no turkeys, cotton candy, melons, or shishkebobs
   As long as you stay within the above guidelines, we

leave the specific choices up to you. However, we do recommend the following recipe:

INGREDIENTS:
½ lb butter
1 box dark brown sugar
3 eggs
3 cups flour
1 teaspoon vanilla extract
2½ teaspoons baking powder
2 jumbo Hershey bars (the kind with the little squares)

Melt the butter and let it cool until you can put your nose in it for three seconds and feel no pain. Stir in the brown sugar. Then add the flour slowly. Beat the eggs and add them one at a time. Add the vanilla and baking powder. Break off the chocolate bars into _____ squares with your _____ and add them to the batter.

(A) bulletproof . . . 12 gauge   (B) little . . . fingers
(C) liquid . . . fly swatter   (D) gaseous . . . squirtgun
(E) atomic-sized . . . nuclear warhead

Answer: (B)

Pour everything into a baking dish with a volume of 216 cubic inches. If it's 2 inches deep and 12 inches long, how many inches wide is it?

(A) 8   (B) 9   (C) 10   (D) 25   (E) $8x - 5$

Answer: (B)

Take a big handful of the batter and eat it. (Don't you wish all recipes said that?) Preheat oven to the average of 100 and 600. It takes 35 minutes for them to turn golden brown in a standard oven. If an oven is slow it takes 40 minutes.

Sweet and Tasty 800 Bars

Quantitative Comparison

Column A	*Column B*
The length of time it takes to turn golden brown in a slow oven.	The length of time given for an SAT math section.

Answer: (A)

When they are golden brown, remove them from the oven. Now you can cut them into whatever shape you choose.

Sneaking Food into the Test Center

If you're taking the test during the winter, it's no problem to get the food in. Just hide it in your coat. Smuggling food to the May and June dates can be trickier. Your best bet is one of those hooded sweatshirts with the pockets in the front. These can hold a lot of food, and the food is easily accessible because it's in your front pocket. Pocketbooks are also useful. Do not do what Larry did. He cleverly concealed a chocolate bar in his back pocket. Before he had a chance to eat it, two of the Musketeers had melted.

PARTING WORDS OF ADVICE
(To Be Read the Night Before the Test)

Congratulations, you've made it through. You know what the word *cerebration* means, and you're all set to be cerebral. You have your ID, your admission ticket, three sharp pencils and one dull pencil, and some food to smuggle into the test all waiting by the door. Maybe you've studied everything in a day; maybe you started with verbal flashcards four and a half years ago. Who cares? It's over now; no amount of studying the night before the test is going to help you significantly. If you need a boost of confidence, just think that there are people out there who will be taking the test tomorrow without having read this book first. (Unthinkable, isn't it?) If you botch the test, you just take it again on the next test date. If you don't get into the college of your choice, you can choose another one that probably doesn't cost as much and has a better football team.

We hope that you enjoyed our book and that you learned a lot. Our objective was to teach you how to take the SAT, but we hope that along the way you learned some stuff that will help you for the rest of your life. You now know a lot of vocabulary words that you didn't know before, you are a more clever test-taker, and you're a better thinker than you used to be.

Last year, the three of us went through the same thing that you are going through right now. There is a lot of pressure. It feels like someone is scratching their fingers on your mental chalkboard.

So, go outside and look at the stars. There are lots of them and they're trillions of miles away. In the Grand Scheme of the Universe, how big a deal can the SAT be? Be chill. You're going to cruise tomorrow. Sit back. You only live once . . . and then, they send you your score report.

Good luck,

Larry, Manek, Paul

Larry, Manek, Paul

P.S. You do know what the word *lamia* means, don't you?

We'll look this one up for you. According to the *American Heritage Dictionary,* it's "a monster represented as a serpent with the head and breasts of a woman reputed to prey upon humans and suck the blood of children." Sweet dreams.

Larry Berger

Larry Berger is a freshman at Yale University, New Haven, Connecticut, where he is studying English. As a senior in high school, he was editor of the school paper, president of the student council, first seed and captain of the tennis team, and lead guitarist in The Generic Band. He is the winner of the Tollerton and Hood Essay Contest, the Lelia E. Tupper Creative Writing Contest, the BOCES Creative Writing Contest, and the Helena Stanton Journalism Award. He expands to three times his normal size when placed in water.

Manek Mistry

Manek is a respectable individual. His respectable accomplishments include earning an Empire State Scholarship of Excellence, the Peabody Award for music, the Robert S. Perry, Jr., Award for English and music, the Ithaca College Mathematics Department Award for math, the Luther Clarke Foster Memorial Award for scholarship, and an Ithaca High School award for science. Manek is also a National Merit Finalist. He is currently studying biology at Cornell University, Ithaca, New York, where he is trying hard not to become a fathead.

Paul Rossi

Paul Rossi has been called many things by many people, but his name really is Paul. He is a Cornell National Scholar and a National Merit Finalist. He also received a New York State Regents Scholarship and the Luella K. Church Memorial Award for leadership, cooperation, integrity, and scholarship. He is the founder of an award-winning newspaper and was a chief judge in Youth Court. Paul plays the guitar, is interested in astronomy and entomology, and was on the Ithaca High School tiddly-winks team (true). He has spent the past year working and studying in Saint-Malo, France. On the whole, he's a nice guy, and we all put up with him.